Woodruff's Guide to

Slavic
Deities

by Patricia Robin Woodruff, PhD

Book cover by Patricia Robin Woodruff. All interior illustrations are from Wikimedia in the public domain or are otherwise credited.

Library of Congress Cataloging-In-Publication Data

Woodruff, Patricia Robin.

Woodruff's Guide to Slavic Deities

ISBN:

1. Nonfiction - Religion - Ancient.2. Nonfiction - Body, Mind & Spirit - General.

Dedicated to the members of The Roots of Slavic Magic Facebook group, as well as my SCW teachers and fellow students.

the "Germanic" Goddess Striga Holda, the Italian witches who are called *strega,* the Romanian *strigoi* and many more connections. In the same way, not much was known about Radagast, but once you understand that his missing partner should be Rada or Radha (as it is written in Sanskrit), much more about the god becomes clear, as you will see.

In the same manner, the mortal followers (priests/priestesses, shamans, druids or witches) as well as the fey servants often bear the name of the God or Goddess they are connected to. So the Goddess Mora has "fairy" *moras* that would seem to be under her domain and her witch followers would also be called *moras.* While Striga has the eerie fey *strzyga* or *strix* (which have gotten maligned through the years) and Veles has the *vile (veela).*

It is from this beginning that the original pair of a Goddess and her God branched into pairs of seasonal deities that traded places with one another through the year. In the herding culture, the year was only divided in half between the beginning of May and the beginning of November.[1] This makes the earliest variation of the deities to be divided between the "white" half of the year and the "black" half of the year, like Bialobog (*bialo* meaning "white") and Chernobog (*cherno* meaning "black") or Devanna (*div* meaning "light") and Marzanna (*mor* or *mar* meaning "dark"). One morphing into the other around the cycle of the year.

3

The lore of them fighting each other for dominance, like the oft repeated story of Perun and Veles stealing each others' wives and cattle is a more "recent" development of the Warrior Culture. Before that, Perun was just another aspect of Veles as they traded places throughout the year. Also, the Goddess holds a *way* more important role than chattel being stolen!

It would seem that when agriculture arose (around 10,000 years ago give or take) some cultures divided the year into three. As the Victorian Doctor Alexander Tille noted in the writing of Tacitus' *Germania* of 98 CE, "[The Slavic/Germanic tribes] do not divide the year into so many seasons as we do. Only winter, spring, and summer have a name and a meaning among them..."[2] This tripartite division of the year was reflected in the deities; giving us the triple goddess and triple god. Contrasted with the herding culture's two-part year, this causes some discrepancies between various cultures' account of which title of the deity was reigning at what time.

This book generally looks at the deities as a triple goddess and triple god as they cycle around the year, being reborn in the spring. They are as different as I was as a child, a mother and now as a priestess. Yet they are also the same deity, just as I am the same person throughout my life. However, deity is not bound by a mortal form and can appear in many

4

different guises. Originally there was no "mother of", "father of" or Slavic Pantheon with a "head god". Those are recent human constructs.

While many researchers have focused specifically on Polish gods or Baltic gods in the pride of nationalism, this indigenous earth religion spanned the entire area from Finland to Persia, from the Atlantic coast to Kazakhstan. It is not until you draw back and look at the big picture that these deities from the Neolithic begin to fall into place.

Another huge component of being able to look at these deities differently came from my realization that the multiplicity of gods arises from the fact that the "true" name of the deity was much too holy to use on a regular basis, so titles were used. It is common knowledge that certain animals had names that were not used so as to not invoke the "magic of the word" to energetically attract their attention. However, this principal seems to have been overlooked by previous researchers when applied to the deities. Once you realize that these are not names but "titles" you can clearly see why there is so much confusion.

These deities have existed for thousands upon thousands of years and just as so many of the different languages stem from Proto-Indo-European (roughly 6,000 years ago), the deities have proliferated throughout many different countries, retaining some qualities and losing others depending on the culture, yet at their core, they remain the same. Just as an apple can be called *appel, epli, pomme, mele* or *jabłko* and is the same fruit. Yet apple varieties can differ widely in different countries and the deities reflect the culture they are worshipped in. To clarify the example I am using, a large green Granny Smith and a small red Pippin vary as much as Perunika and Brigid do but they are essentially the same goddess.

Although not much on Slavic deities was written down (and what was written was mainly by the priests of an antithetical religion) we can tell the deities' qualities based on their descriptive titles. Additional clues can be gathered based on plant names that are still used. For example, mugwort provides a connection between the Greek goddess Artemis and the Slavic goddess known as Siva or Vida. Mugwort's Latin name is *Artemisia vulgaris* but in Slovenia its folk name is *Vidina zel* meaning "Vida's herb." When we compare cultures we see the same beliefs surrounding the uses of mugwort and strikingly similar qualities in these goddesses.

This is just a quick summary for those who want to get to know the deities and how to honor them. This book is the culmination of my reading over 300 books, 4,000 research papers, and journeys to Slavic sacred sites, yet there are many more papers in various languages still unread.

Since it hasn't been possible for me to learn all the languages of all the countries I am researching, I apologize if I have made any mistakes with plurals or pronunciation and would appreciate any linguistic correction for future editions. I believe my conclusions are sound based on the information I have, however, I am still researching and my conclusions may change.

Because this is a shorter book I can't include all of the proof that I have gathered, if this contradicts something you have learned already, I ask you to wait until after reading all my sources in the Roots of Slavic Magic series. I feel that I have been led by the Divine in my research and hopefully their message has been accurately conveyed through me.
    - Patricia Robin Woodruff, PhD

Woodruff's Guide to Slavic Deities

TITLES OF DEITIES

Bialobog and Czarnobog seem to divide the year into two and may be titles used in the transhumant pastoral cultures.

SPRING
Vesna and Kresnik (Vesnik)
Radagast (Svarozic) and Rada
Lada and Lado
Jarila and Jarilo
Austeja and Auseklis (Ūsiņš)
Devana
Dazbog

SUMMER
Perunika (Perperuna) and Perun
Siva and Seibog (Svarog)
Vit (Svantovit) and Vita
Kupala and Kupalo

WINTER
Mora and Hors (Hors-Dazbog)
Korent and Korencia
Mat Zemla and Zemepattys
Veles and Veliona
Baba Yaga and Koshchei the Deathless
Stribog and Striga
Zozim (Babilos) and Zize
Koliada and Koliado

UNDEFINED
(I suspect that Berehynia may be just another title of Perunika, but this has to be confirmed [or denied] with further research, so for now I will leave Mokosh and Berehynia in their own category.)

Mokosh
Berehynia

TRIPLE GODDESS & GOD
(These deities can be seen as both a singular entity or in their triple form.)

Triglava and Triglav
Rozhanitsa and Rod

Bialobog (bee-AH-LOO-boog) "The White

God" (Bel, Belboch, Bel Bog, Belbog, Belboh,
Belbuck, Belbuk, Beli Bog, Belibog, Belin, Belinez,
Belinus, Belobog, Belun, Bely Bogue, Belye Bogi,
Bialun, Biel, Biel-Bog, Bielbog, Bielobog, Bielboh,
Bielun, Biełunem, Byelin, Byelobog, Byeluie Bogi,
Byelbozhsky, Bylun, Dzied, Gilbog, Niebo, Velibog,
Veli-bogc)

The first written source of information on "Bielbog"
came from Thomas Kantzow in 1538:
"They also worshipped the sun and the moon and
two gods to whom they assigned a higher value than
to other gods. One they called Bialbug- that is the
white god, believing him to be a good god, the other
Zernebug- that is the black god, believing him to be a
god who did harm. Therefore, they honored Bialbug
so that he should do them good, and Zernebug so
that he should not harm them…"[3] However, this
was written by a dualistic Christian. To the
indigenous people a "good" god and "evil" god
makes as much sense as a "good" fire or an "evil"
fire. It just is, but you would want to protect yourself
from unwanted effects.

Bialobog is a manifestation of the God of the Life-
Bringing Radiance during the "white" summertime of
the year. In Poland, in a book from 1885, they write,
"The white god, as he was commonly called, and
who Belorussians today call Biełunem, was
considered by all Slavic tribes as the master of

11

heaven, and his wife was Diva..."[4] [Further in this book you'll find that Diva is also known as Siva, Zhiva, Vita, etc. She is the Radiant White Goddess.] The Belorussians envision him with a fair beard wearing white clothing.[5]

In Slovenian oral tradition the god Belin became "St. Belinus" who was a powerful healer. The White Russians (Lemko) knew him as Byelun and described him thus: "[he was] represented as an old man with a long white beard, dressed in white, and carrying a staff in his hand, who appears only by day, and who assists travelers to find their way out of the dark forests. He is the bestower of wealth and fertility, and at harvest time he often appears in the grain fields, and assists the reapers."[6]

Henbane may have been used by his shamanic followers as a way to connect ecstatically to the god, as it has hallucinogenic properties and carries the name of *belena or beleno*.[7]

Tolkien may have modeled his Gandalf the White on this god, since he is full of light, warmth, life, and creativity. His focus is external. He is logical but also full of joy. He is a healer and shapes the life energy as needed. His focus is on helping others and is external: guiding the lost, giving to the poor, aiding the sick, caring for children, helping things grow, aiding one's efforts. He is a radiant, merry god of light and energy.

Followers: *belici*
Sacred Day, Time or Holiday: summertime of the year from Cross Quarter day May 4-7 to November 5-8, alternately from the Winter Solstice to the Summer Solstice.
Sacred Space: top of hills
Sacred Animals: horses (especially white)
Sacred Plants: daisy, white or yellow flowers, henbane
Sacred Objects: white, golden or copper objects, wheel, sun symbols
Offerings: gold or copper, eggs

"The Stone of Krkavče" with a radiant deity which some say depicts "Belin" now located by a roadside in Koper, Slovenia (exact original site unknown). Approximately 2,000 to 3,000 years old. Historian Boris Čok states that the "Old Believers" worshipped by it in secret, laying hands on it on the feast day of St. Vida (June 15, essentially the Summer Solstice) and burning a sacred log at Christmas (Winter Solstice).
Source: Photo by Patricia Robin Woodruff 2018.

Czarnobog (shchar-NOO-boog) "The Black-God" (Čarnaboh, Cerni Bog, Chernabog, Chornbog, Cherno-Bog, Chornoboh, Crn, Crnobog, Czarnoglowy, Czernabog, Drognjuš, Tchernobog, Tcherny Bogue, Tjarnaglofi, Tschernebog, Tsernobog, Zarneboch, Zcerneboch, Zernebock, Zernebok, Zernebuck, Zerne-Bog, Zerneboh, Zernebug, Ziemobogowi, Zlebog) -

He is known as the "Black God" (*chorna, czarna, zerni, zrini*, all meaning "black.")[8] His reign is about October 26th/November 8th until he "dies" and is transformed to Bialabog on May 6th. It is said that Chernobog can shape change to a black dog.[9] James Cowles Prichard writes, "Czerno-bogc, or Tschernebog, was represented even in the temples of the Wends on the Baltic, a circumstance which points to their Asiatic origin, under the figure of a lion."[10] [However, an "Asiatic origin" is counter-indicated by the evolution of languages. Additionally, Asia is not the only place to find lions since they still inhabited the European Caucasus until the 10th century!][11] However, this lets us know that Czarnobog was envisioned as transforming into a lion, which connects him to depictions of the Master of the Animals. This *might* even connect Czarnobog to depictions of the 32,000 year old "Lion Man" sculpted out of mammoth ivory found in Hohlenstrein-Stadel, Germany. Researcher Goran Pavlovic points out that a folk painting of a cockerel and lion found in the Kirovsky Museum of History in

Russia might symbolize the transition of summer animal/god to winter animal/god.[12]

The same sacred place, the top of a hill, was sacred to both Bialobog and Czarnobog, showing Czarnobog is not only a god of the underworld, but the God of the Life-Bringing Radiance during the "black" wintertime of the year. In Belarus, Čarnaboh is married to Marana, the goddess of death,[5] which shows he is the winter form of the God of Radiant Light with his partner, Marana/Mora. He is depicted as having a black head and silver mustache.

Czarnobog is master of the animals symbolized by the lion, the "King of the Animals." After the extinction of the lion Czarnobog's lore then became focused on him being master of the wolves. He keeps the balance of the animals and decides which is to die.

The dark haired Czarnobog is focused inward and encourages being intuitive. He loves the dark, cold, and stillness. He is the lord of death and rest. He disassembles life energy, yet he is also brings brings forth the possibility of renewal. The natural progression of nature decomposing, breaking down into smaller parts, yet still holding that life-force, ready to be reassembled into a new shape. His focus is the internal processes and introspection. He helps those who are called to the magical arts to work with their shadow-selves and understand their own internal motivations.

Followers: *zernici, chernoknizhnik* are considered "black magicians" casting harmful spells, but whether they get their name from this god or from the concept of being "evil" magicians is unclear.

Sacred Day, Time or Holiday: winter time of the year from Cross Quarter day November 5-8 to May 4-7, or alternatively from Summer Solstice to the Winter Solstice.

Sacred Space: top of hills and caves

Sacred Animals: dogs, wolves, lions, mice

Sacred Plants: holly, mushrooms

Sacred Objects: black

Offerings: black objects, minerals, root vegetables, bread or honey cakes

Lion on a Macedonian coat of arms by Peter
Ohmucevic.

SPRING

Vesna (VEES-nah) "Lady Spring", "Lady of Spring Resurrection" or "The White Maiden of May"- (Alenčica, Deva, Kresnica, Kresnika,Maja Zlatogorka, Marjetica, Mara, Mare, Mari, Maya, Vesina, Wesna, Zlatogorka, Zlata Maja, Zora)

The spring goddess' title goes back to the proto-Slavic word *vesna* derived from the Proto-Indo-European *wésr₀* meaning "spring."[13] Her name of Zlata Maja means **"Golden Mother of Life"** and Zlatogorka means **"Golden Hill."** As Marjetica her name means **"Daisy."**[14] The daisy is also the flower sacred to Freya, the Radiant Goddess of the Norse and it means "day's-eye".[15] She is a glowing, radiant goddess described as having long golden hair.[16] Vesna is also associated with the day that the swallows return on March 9th called *Strinenija*. At this point in the year, Striga/Mora/Morana would be reborn as the spring goddess Vesna. The dates would vary based on climatic differences in the various Slavic countries.

In Slovenia, she is also called Maya, described by Dr. Šavli as the "goddess of nature, greenery and flowers and gave her name to the month May."[17] On the first of May she is crowned with flowers, a tradition carried on in the Roman Catholic church with the

May crowning of Virgin Mary. But Vesna is not a virgin and revels in her sexuality along with all nature.

We see Edwardian writer, E. Richmond Hodges writing about the goddess in 1875 that, "She was worshipped by the Polabes under the name of Siva, a beautiful maiden, represented as naked, her hair flowing down to her heels; she holds her hands behind her back; in one hand she holds a golden apple, and in the other a bunch of grapes with a green leaf. Her head is crowned with flowers: and, as goddess of birth and death, she bears the twofold name of Wesna [sic] and Morana."[18] So, this either means that Vesna is the same as Siva, and Morana is her winter form, or that Vesna, Siva and Morana are the names of the triple goddess; Maiden, Mother and Crone.

She loves music, song and dance, as well as making love and sensual pleasures. She bedecks herself with a flower crown and the land with beautiful flowers. She might be found naked dancing in a meadow with her long hair rippling in the breeze, happily surrounded by birds and butterflies. Like all the tales of the Slavic Gods, she can change her shape and turn herself into the animals she mosts connects with such as a white bird, rabbit or singing lark. These are her messengers.

Her lovely fairy servants are called *vesna* or *vesnar*. They are also naked or clad in white, who dance around awakening spring and bringing fertility.[19]

Followers: *Vesna, Vesnar, Vesne* or mortal females by the name of *Kresnice* or *Ladarice*
Sacred Day, Time or Holiday: Fridays, the month of May but especially May Day
Sacred Space: flowery meadows, gardens, hills
Sacred Animals: white birds, larks, rooks, robins, cranes, mice, shrews, cuckoos, fireflies & glow worms
Sacred Plants: lily-of-the-valley, daisies, maple, beech, hawthorn blossoms, wild roses
Sacred Objects: window quartz, spindle, yarn
Offerings: honey cakes, flowers, apples, goat's milk, bird sculptures especially spring birds (larks, rooks, robins, cranes, cuckoos), yarn, flower crowns

A lady with an apple by Emily J. Harding 1896

Kresnik (kre-ES-nik) "Living Fire", "Lord of Spring Resurrection", "The Lord of Life-Giving Light" - (Bergant, Erich, Erlik, Kersnik, Krstnik, Skrstnik, Vedogonja, Vesnič, Vesnik, Vedogonja, Zeleni Jurij) -

In Slovene, *kresati* means to kindle a fire by striking, essentially "living fire."[19] A bonfire is also known as a *kres*.[17] Interestingly enough, *kres* can also mean "a change of time (season)"[14] and we see bonfires in *all* of the celebrations marking the Solstices, Equinoxes and Cross-Quarter days. We also see the god connected with time-keeping.

Folklorist F. S. Copeland interprets Kresnik's name Skrstnik to mean **"Resurrector"** and his cognomen of Obilnjak means **"Giver of Plenty"**. While his name, Zeleni Jurij means **"Green George,"**[14] the same as St. George or Jarilo. He is the origin of the European Green Man.

In folktales, Kresnik can transform into a bird and fly, turn into any shape he pleases as well as become invisible. He rides in a golden carriage across the sky or on a winged horse. We see him in Slovene folk tales as wielding a "golden axe" and causing lightning.

Kresnik is bright and radiantly handsome with golden hair, a golden mustache, and golden hands (and sometimes wings). He lives on a golden mountain where there grows an apple tree with the golden apples of immortality. In tales he is described as a prince/shaman/sorcerer holding protective powers of magic for his land. In the tale our hero is described with a mustache of gold, eyes like a falcon, eyebrows like sable's fur and a right hand of pure gold. "His manner and appearance were so full of an indescribable majesty, that he was looked upon by everyone with a feeling of awe."[16]

His partner has various titles: Alenčica, Maya, Mari, Mara, Marjetica, Zora, Deva and Vesina. She is the goddess of May, Vesina (Vesna) who is also his twin. [20] In folktales from Slovenia, Kresnik can transform into a bird and fly (or just sprout wings). In other tales, he can turn into any shape he pleases as well as become invisible.[14] He has appeared as a red cow, a sow with horses' hooves, a horse, donkey, or an ox.[21] One can also become a *kresnik*, a type of shamanic worker who journeys while "asleep" as a spirit or a lynx. These shamanic workers are said to hunt vampires and protect their village from malicious spirits.

The firefly (lightning bug) is sacred to Kresnik. His abode lies in the East, in "the Land of the Rising Sun".[20] He is remembered in India as the young, handsome god Krishna.

Followers: *kresniki* (m) or *kresnice* (f) Another name is *sentjanjevec* or *Šentjanževci* (pl), but this is a Christianized intermediate form, since it is describing a magic worker who works with *Sentjanjevec*, "the one who manifests on St. John's Day."

Sacred Day, Time or Holiday: Spring Equinox, May 6th, Summer Solstice (June 21 or 22), November 11th (although more accurately Nov. 7th or October 31st) December 6th, & the Winter Solstice. The winter Solstice was considered his "birthday" and then he was celebrated at the Summer Solstice with bonfires.

Sacred Space: hill

Sacred Animals: roosters, goats, red cows, bulls, bears, wolves, boars, oxen, dragons, horse, flying horse, dogs with white spots over their eyes, woodpeckers, lynxes, fireflies & glow worms

Sacred Plants: apples, yellow "Corn Marigolds," grapevines, buckwheat, blackberries, red cranberries, asparagus, hay, wheat, fruit

Sacred Objects: spoked "sun wheels", flute, fiddle, a golden hand, a winged white horse, a candelabrum, golden axe, club

Offerings: golden apples, wine, cooked buckwheat, grapes, cranberries, wheat sheaves, candles, incense, Frankincense

"Obhod Zelenega Jurija na Štajerskem"
(A procession of "Green George" in Styria)
by Jurij Šubic 1890

Radagast (rah-dah-GHAST) "The Ploughing One" "The Hospitable One" "The Peacemaker" "The Revolving Wheel" (Badegast, Gadebusz, Krišnji, Kryshen, Radagais, Radagoszcz, Radegast, Radegastus, Radgosc, Radgost, Radgostor, Radhost, Radigast, Radigost, Radoist, Radogosc, Radogost, Radomysl', Radovit, Redigast, Redigost, Riedegost, Suarasiz, Svarozhich, Svarozic, Svarozich, Svorozic, Swarozyc, Swarozycze, Tvarozic, Zuarasici, Zuarasiz, ZvaigždikasZuarasiz, Zyzal)

In a book from 1722 which included a work from 1710 by M. Stredowsky who wrote *The Sacred History of Moravia* included the following description, "The Moravians worshipped under that name King Radagaisus, who brought into Italy in the year 405 an army of 400,000 men and was defeated by Stilicon. His statue was made of gold. He had a majestic look and wore a crown of an unknown metal, covered with a bird stretching its wings. There was on his breast a head of a black bull, which he held up with his right hand, and he had an ax in the left. A stately bed lay by him. His temple was upon Mount Radhost, near the head of the river Beczua."[22] [King Radagaisus was named for Radagast and was conflated with the worship of the god.]

RADEGAST

"Radegast" by Bernard de Montfaucon 1722

There is also an illuminated manuscript dated around 1530 entitled *"Radegast zu Mecklenburg und andere slawische Götter"* (Radegast of Mecklenburg and other Slavic Gods) which includes a figure very similar to this.

In another rare description of "Radegast" by E. Richmond Hodges in 1875, "His image was of gold, his couch of purple, his hair curled and arranged in a circle; on his head a bird stood with outspread wings, and on his breast the head of a black ox supported by the right hand, the left hand holding a double axe." People would come to his temple to bring offerings and ask for divination.[23]

In the Czech Republic *radlo* means "plough" and its pronunciation is compared to "early Slavic borrowings in neighbouring [sic] languages, e.g. Radogost."[24] Linguist Davorin Trstenjak saw the name Radogost as essentially the same as Kurent, "the ploughman" linked with the young, fertile, spring Lord of the Radiant Light.[25] Słupecki concludes that "Radogost would be a local nickname of Svorozic, used in his sanctuary."[23] In an old Polish book from 1885, they concluded the same thing, that "Swarozycze" was the same as "Badegast" [sic] and known to the Belarusians as Zyzal. They called him the "king of fire." So Radagast could be the "same god as the warrior, Swarozyc" in the spring version of Seibog/Vit, but in a later form as a warrior god.

Radagast's title of Svarozic is a diminutive of Svarog. This makes him a spring version of the summer god Svarog. In the same way, the diminutive of the Yule log, Badgnak, is Božic. Ivan Navratil noted that the term *božič* denotes a young or small god (Navratil 1848: 203-204). Niko Kuret suggested that the origin

29

of Božič may be in the period of the Old Slavs, when he represented a young (small) god by the name Svarožič. Like the Green Dionysus, god of agriculture, Svarog was allegedly born, each year anew on the winter solstice. Shortened into the name Božič, the name of the young god Svarožič was allegedly transferred to the new-born Christian saviour when the population living in the territory of present day Slovenia embraced Christianity…" In Slovenia, Božic means "god-child" and is what they call Christmas day. The name Božic is of pre-Christian origin and connects to Kresnik, the God of Life-Bringing Light who is celebrated on the Spring Equinox, May Day and the Summer Solstice.[17] In Slovenia they would celebrate the Winter Solstice with a huge bonfire in honor of the god, which has morphed to just the *božic* or "Yule log." Here we see that Svarozic, Kresnik, Radagast, Zyzal and Bozic are all different titles of the young spring god.

Just as the young radiant god Apollo grew up fast and so did Kresnik, this young god child becomes a young man by the time of the spring celebration. Svarozic is mentioned as "Zuarasici" in the writings of Thietmar of Merseburg circa 1,000 CE and as "Zuarasiz diabolus" by Bruno of Querfurt in 1008 CE. In Croatian fairy tales Svarožič is translated as "All-Rosy" or "All-Rose" because he is the bright shining youth of spring and dawn and the east.[26]

An additional little tidbit that might confirm Radagast as being a spring incarnation of the god is found in Russian folk tales where Dazbog married Zlatogorka. Her unmelodic name actually means "The Golden Hill," or essentially the "Radiant Goddess of Summer". Zlatogorka bore a daughter Koljada, which would be the young Goddess of the New Year. She married Radimicu (presumably another title for Koliado) and they had a son, "Radogost."[27] Thus making Radagast the Lord of Spring.

Researcher, A. Von Ulrich writes in 1907, "In Rugen the same god [as Svantovit] with the same attributes was called Rugiaevit, and had other names in other districts, according to the people whom he protected. Thus in the town of Rethru he was called Radagais, which means in Lithuanian, the "Revolving Wheel," a very suitable name for a sun-god. The chroniclers also use the form Radigost, which is probably a bad spelling of the former. In another place he is called Gadebusz, which means Peacemaker." Ulrich goes on to explain, this is because the god would resolve disputes in the following manner: "[the xoanon] held a strangely-shaped iron instrument in his hand, called a proving-iron, which served to demonstrate guilt or innocence. It was heated red-hot, and taken in the hand, and if the person was innocent he received no harm from it. This god wore a gold crown, with erect rays, and was called Gadebusz = Peacemaker..."[28] (This "proving-iron" may have been a double axe or shaped like the Indian symbol of the lightning bolt, the *vajra*.) We can see the ox, symbol of the Lord of Radiant Light, as well as his "halo" of curly hair.

Another tiny clue comes from the Serbian celebration of the Winter Solstice, where a handsome youth sets "first foot" in the house on the Solstice morning. Presumably this boy or young man represents the young radiant god who is reborn. He is supposed to be the first person who steps foot inside the house, and he brings a gift of grain. This boy is usually called a *polznik*, but sometimes called *radovan*.[29]

Followers: *radovan* or *redari*
Sacred Day, Time or Holiday: the first day of the "new year" (Winter Solstice day, Spring Equinox, May Day), spring and summer
Sacred Space: hills, by water
Sacred Animals: ox or cattle, eagle or falcon
Sacred Plants: sun-shaped flowers
Sacred Objects: the offering dish, flute, *vajra* (thunderbolt), radiant gold crown, golden objects, sacred fire, double axe, golden wheel
Offerings: fire, sunny flowers, golden crown of flowers, grain

"Radegast" by Andrej S. Kajsarov from the Versuch diner Slavischen Mythologie.

"Radegast" by Franciszek Piekosiński - 1896
This is an illustration of one of the bronze Prillwitz
Idols labeled "Radegast" discovered in the late 17th
Century however their authenticity is still in doubt.

Rada - (rah-DAH)"The Grower" "Fate" (Radha, Rhode, Rhodos)

In Slavic lore, Rada is mainly forgotten. Yet, once we know that Radagast is the young Lord of Spring and there is a hole where his partner should be let us see where we find Rada...

The first place you might find her is in India under the name Radha, the young Goddess of Love. There she is a lover of Krishna (which I have just mentioned is the same as Kresnik, the Spring God.) Then when we take a peek back at Slavic lore we see a mention of Rada as the "daughter of the Sun" married to the obscure Slavic god Krišnji or Kryshen.[30] While this is a recent reconstruction, it verifies that others have seen the same connection, although they didn't see where it connected with Radagast.

The India Goddess Radha is seen with the sacred cow. It's especially exciting to see that the Hindus celebrate the sacred dance of Rada & Radagast aka Vesna and Vesnik/Kresnik, etc. In India it is called the *Raslila* dance, where maidens dance in a circle just as Radha and her cow herders danced to Krishna's piping. This shows a connection to the circle dances performed by Slavic maidens held during *Rusalii*. This indicates that Rada and Radagast are Lord and Lady over the Slavic fey that live by and in the water, the *Rusalka*. One of the holy sites where Radha and Krishna are supposed to dance each night is located in the sacred town of Vrindavan, India (which when you remove the "V" looks like the Serbian *radovan* who is the young man representing the god of the new year. *Radovan* stepping across the threshold on the first day of the new year (Kupala) brings luck and prosperity to the home.)

There is a good possibility that the goddess Hreda, (Hrede, Hretha) mentioned by Bede as the goddess of March was an Anglo-Saxon version of Rada. There is no other mention of this goddess except that the tribe name of Hreðgotan (Reiðgotan) means "Hreda's Goths". Bede also mentions Eostre, the goddess of April, whom I can definitively connect to the Slavic Goddess of Spring. Jacob Grimm derives Hrede from Hruod or Hruodâ which he theorizes that it derives "from *hruod gloria, fama*[fame]; so that we get the meaning of a shining and renownful [sic] goddess." Author Phillip Shaw suggests a connection to Hreðon meaning "rejoicing".[31]

There is also the Greek Goddess Rhodos from whom the island of Rhodes was named. There she is described as a "sea Nymph" who was the "consort of the sun god Apollo".[32] The Greek lore has her with seven sons called the *Kouretes*. These *Kouretes* were said to be gods of the wild, "inventors of the rustic arts of metalworking, shepherding, hunting and beekeeping."[33] In the Slavic lands, these *Kouretes* are also called *Korebantes, Kurenti, Kukeri, Caretos,* and *Călușari* and they appear at the "new year" celebrations. This name is carried by the mortal participants in the Carnival parades. Dressing in fur, ribbons or tatters, often wearing horns and clanking and jingling bells, they represent the fey servants of the Horned God. They carry on the traditions of their shamanic forebears: chasing away winter, welcoming the spring, increasing fertility and performing healing rituals.

The origin of Rada's name may be from the Proto-Indo-European word *$Hreh_1d^h$*, which has come to mean "to grow" or "to increase". While in the Gothic language it became "to predestine," essentially Fate.

Followers: *radovan* or *redari, Rusalki*
Sacred Day, Time or Holiday: the first day of the "new year" (Winter Solstice day, Spring Equinox, May Day), spring and summer
Sacred Space: hills, by water
Sacred Animals: cow or cattle, eagle or falcon
Sacred Plants: sun-shaped flowers, roses
Sacred Objects: the offering dish, flute, radiant gold crown, golden objects, sacred fire
Offerings: fire, sunny flowers, golden crown of flowers, grain, dance and song

Radha and Krishna dancing the Rasalila - 19th
century by anonymous artist.

Lada (lad-DAH) "Lady" or "Queen" or "The Young Maiden of Love and Fertility" (Daźba, Dachuba, Daszuba, Dida, Didilela, Didilya, Djedijielia, Doda, Dodol, Dodola, Dola, Dudulya, Dudylya, Dzidzileyla, Kolita, Kostroma, Ladana, Ladja, Lala, Leda, Lejla, Lela, Lelia, Lelika, Lelja, Lelya, Lejia, Lel, Lele, Leli, Leliu, Liada, Lila, Liljana, Liola, Liuli, Ljelije, Ljelje, Lola, Lyalya, Lyolya, Niwa Manzena, Pilwis, Pilwite, Poljelja, Sotwora, Sweigsdunka, Sweigsdonoka, Veleda, Walada, Yleli, Zezylia, Zimtserla, Zizilia, Zyzylas) -

Lada can mean "joy" while her name variation of Lila means "love." Other variations of her name give her the title of **"Great Lady"** or **"Queen/Heiress."**[34] Lada is recorded as the goddess of love and springtime, fertility and marriage. Lada and Lado bestow their love and blessings on handfastings and weddings. Since they are also fertility deities of the fields and grain, this is where we get the traditions of tossing rice (grain) on the married couple to convey fertility. There is also a Slavic tradition of the bride tossing some of her wine up into the air as an offering for the goddess of love.

In an old Byelorussian song there is a reference to the "goddess of Spring Lada-Liola."[5] Some colloquial expressions allude to the cult of Lada: in Volhynia *"laduvaty"* means to conduct a wedding, and in Transcarpathia and the Presov region *"ladkanky"* are wedding songs, and *"ladkaty"* is to sing wedding songs."[35] So Lada and Lado bestow their love and blessings on handfastings and weddings.

In Lithuania, Lada is remembered as the goddess of fortune and one's fate. She is **"Lady Luck."** Just like Vesna, the worship of Lada was transferred to the worship of the Virgin Mary along with Lada's title of "May Queen" and her crown of roses. Lada is much more sexual than the Christian Mary, causing her name to be used for the "women of the evening" in Rome called *lella*.[36] Lada's loving and sexual nature is healthy and joyous bringing fertility to the earth. Lada is also associated with the *gwiazda/rozeta* - protective rosettes carved in wood."[34] In Belarus, Lada had her feast on the day before her partner. It used to be April 22, which in the Gregorian calendar would be May 4th. Lada's feast was called *Lalnik*, and the following day was *Jaryly*, the festival of Jarilo on May 5th.[4] [Another small confirmation that Lado is just another title for Jarilo.] This is right around the Cross Quarter day and Celtic Beltane. A celebration of the fertility of the land and the love of the Spring God and Goddess.

In Lithuania, they have used the title of Triwejde Lele Kunigie, indicating that Lela is the youthful form of the triple-goddess.[36] In her triple form, she presides over the birth, life and death of man. In Lithuania, she is remembered as the goddess of fortune and one's fate (like Siva.)

Followers: *ladarice* (f)
Sacred Day, Time or Holiday: Fridays, March 30 (or Spring Equinox) May Day to Summer Solstice
Sacred Space: bright, open wind-swept hills with water nearby
Sacred Animals: crane, swallows, lark, white swan, white birds, deer, ant
Sacred Plants: lime tree (linden), birch, cherry trees, wild geranium (cranesbill geranium), the legendary blooming fern, lily (specifically Turk's cap a/k/a martagon lily), Guelder-rose, roses (Viburnum) or wild rose, peony, ivy, basil, hawthorn blossoms, maidenhair fern, willow
Sacred Objects: flowers, figures of birds, flute, the planet Venus
Offerings: honey, berries, apples, flower wreaths, white cock, paper-cut of "Tree of Life" known as a *leluja*
Symbol: six-petaled rosette

"Veleda" by Juan Scherr 1882

"Leluja" Tree of Life paper cutout by anonymous
artist

"Watering of Dodola" by Uroš Predić 1892

Lado (lah-DOH) - "Great Lord" "The Lover" or "The Young Lord of Love and Fertility" (Boshizh, Božič, Dide, Dido, Did-Lado, Didzis Lado, Dzidzis Lado, Kostromo, Lad, Ladon, Lados, Laduno, Lel, Laduno, Svarozhich, Savarozic, Sorvaras Purškio, Sotvaras, Sotwar, Sotwaros,Svarozic, Svarozich, Swarozyc, Tvarozic, Zuarasici, Zuarasiz, Zvaigždikas)

Dido, means "great" and is usually used in conjunction with Lado, while the word *lado* is the term for a lover in Russian ballads.[37] He is mentioned in conjunction with the spring and sun, "Lado, O Sun, Lado."[6] Lado is mentioned as 'The God of marriage, of mirth, of pleasure, and of general happiness,' to whom those who were about to marry offered sacrifices, in order to secure a fortunate union."[6] Since it's kind of hard to have a marriage with just one person, the same thing is said about Lada. Yet, they existed long before the institution of marriage, so it is more accurate to look upon them as the deities of "mutual love" and fertility. His title of Sotwaros, has its Lithuanian variation of Sotvaras, where he is known as the "god of daylight".[38] (Remember that Radagast has also been connected to Sotvaras.)

In Lithuania he is connected with the plant known as bog myrtle, a traditional flavoring for beer. Beer is one of the mind-altering substances that was used to reach an altered state where one could be receptive to the message of the god.

45

In Belarusian lore, they remembered "Lad" as "a god of spring, love, marriage and grace."[5] But they forgot that he was the partner of Lada, and instead she is paired with the god in his form as "Dažboh" since they were both mentioned at the Summer Solstice. This is one of the transition dates when Lado and Lada would transform into Hors-Dažboh and Mora/Dziva for the Autumn/Winter time of the year.

Lado is depicted as a happy, golden-haired youth dressed in white, surrounded by flowers and all the symbols of spring. Wearing a crown of flowers or ivy, he frolics over the spring meadows. Sometimes he is accompanied by his celestial partner Lada and they sing, dance and play music together. They are said to particularly enjoy playing the flute, called a *svirel* (also called *soplika* or *tsevnitsa*.)[39] It was made out of a birch branch, their sacred tree. They bless all young lovers with delight and pleasure; whether it be the mutual joy of the moment and gentle parting, in a temporary handfasting or in marriage. Lado extends "peace, union and harmony" on all mutual loving relationships. He is also a healing god. His symbol is a six-pointed sun/star and a crescent moon, showing his connection with the radiant bodies of the heavens.[36]

Sacred Day, Time or Holiday: May Day to Summer Solstice

Sacred Space: bright, open windswept hills with water nearby
Sacred Animals: white cock
Sacred Plants: lime tree, birch tree, wild geraniums (cranesbill geranium), the legendary blooming fern, ivy, asparagus, bog myrtle
Sacred Objects: ribbons, flowers, wedding bells, handfasting ribbon or cloth, sex toys, flute
Offerings: apples, flower wreaths, honey, gold and golden things, white cock, beer
Symbol: Six-pointed sun/star and crescent moon

"Leliwa Coat of Arms" 1572

LUBLINIANIE W DZIEŃ WESELNY.

PAYNANS POLONAIS DES ENVIRONS DE LUBLIN. | POLNISCHE LANDLEUTE aus der GEGEND von LUBLIN.
le jour de la noce.   am Tage der Hochzeit.

POLISH PEASANTS IN THE NEIGHBOURHOOD OF LUBLIN
on the Wedding day.

"Polish Peasants in the Neighbourhood of Lublin on
the Wedding Day" by Leon Zienkowicz 1841

Jarila - (yahr-ILL-ah) "The Young Maiden of Spring, Fertility and Life Giving Water" "The Shining Goddess" (Dyza, Dysza, Iarila, Germania, Grubite, Iutroboh, Jana, Jastarnia, Jelena, Jelica, Jumala, Juternica, Juterniza, Jutrzenka, Melitele, Milusienka, Ostara, Pergrubie, Yara, Yarila, Yuternica)

In Latvia, the divine spring couple is known as Jumis and Jumala and connected to the fertility of the grain. [40] Her and her partner Jarilo have lore connected to the May Day festival. She is depicted nude and crowned with flowers, or dressed completely in flowers and greenery. Much of her worship was subsumed by her partner, but she is the watery aspect of this Water & Fire festival. She is also a healer. She is the goddess of the East, where the sun rises, and along with being the goddess of spring, she is also the goddess of the dawn.[41]

In the blog, "In Nomine Jasse," the author mentions the Linde Dictionary by Samuel Bogumil Linde, which lists the town "Iuterbok - [a] Serbian town within the borders of Lower Susatia, so called after Iutroboh, that is the Goddess of dawn, who the Sorbs counted among their Gods."[41] Her alternate name of Juternica, meaning the "Shining Goddess," would seem to connect to the Wendish Juterniza and *jutrzenka* which is Polish for "dawn" and "morning star." [42] The previous name for Jastarnia, Poland was Osternesse, showing her worshipped there under the Germanic name of Ostara, from which we get the name of the holiday of Easter.

In Lithuania, she is known as Pergrubie or Grubite, which comes from *grubios*, a flower and fruit garden. While in Latvia, she was sometimes called Dyza or Dysza and the ancient Prussians called her Melitele. [36] Her Latvian name is connected to the Hebrew name Diza meaning "one who brings joy."[43] She may have given her name to the Hindu earth goddess Diti or Dytea.

Jarila and Jarilo are connected to the direction of East, so prayers are addressed facing that direction. The East being the direction of beginnings, dawn and spring. This connects her with Venus, the Morning Star. Jarila is the joyful Goddess of love, sex, spring, dawn, rebirth and the rising sun. She loves dance and song and flowers. She is described as "a young and beautiful virgin, naked, with her hair loose, reaching below her knees, a wreath of flowers on her head, an apple in her right hand, a wine bunch [of grapes] in her left."[36]

Followers: could be *Căluşari, Kalushari, Waydlot* or *Vaidilos*
Sacred Day, Time or Holiday: May Day to Summer Solstice
Sacred Space: bright, open wind-swept hills with water nearby

Sacred Animals: white birds, chamois goat with golden horns

Sacred Plants: linden (lime) tree, wild geraniums (cranesbill geranium), the legendary blooming fern, ivy, purple loosestrife, roses, the hawthorn blossom

Sacred Objects: ribbons, flowers, wedding bells, handfasting ribbon or cloth, sex toys

Offerings: apples, grapes, flower wreaths, honey, gold and golden things, white birds, rainwater, fresh spring water

"Town of Zinna (now part of Jüterbog) Coat of Arms" showing the fertility goddess, Jarila/Juternica.

"Ostara" by unknown artist 19th century.

Jarilo (yahr-ILL-oh) "Lord of Life", "Lord of Spring" or "The Young Lord of Love, Fertility and Life-Giving Light" (Caloian, Dajbogec, Djurdjev, Djerman, Đorđe, Dzarowit, Egorij, Ger, Georgij, Gergi, Gergio, German, Gerovit, Gerovitus, Gyorgi, Herman, Herovith, Herowit, Janis, Iarilo, Iarovit, Iuru, Iutroboh, Jarego, Jaril, Jarnik, Jarovit, Jarowit, Jarun, Jaryla, Jaryło, Jasny, Jassa, Jastar, Jastër, Jasterbog, Jastrebog, Jastrzëbóg, Jessa, Jesse, Jeou, Jeu, Jore, Jores, Joris, Juma, Jumis, Jura, Juraj, Jurij, Jurgi, Jūrģis, Jüterbog, Jutribog, Kaloian, Kalojan, Kaloyan, Karovit, Kaupolis, K'op'ala, Kostrobunko, Kostrubonko, Kostromo, Peludi-Aika, Patrimp, Potrimppo, Skaloian, Trimpos, Ure, Verowit, Yarilo, Yarily, Yaro, Yarovit, Yarylo, Yuriy, Yur'ya, Yassa, Yasse, Yutribog, Zeleni Juraj, Zeleni Jurij, Zharovit)

Jarilo is the fertile male force of spring. He is described by Leu Horosko as "the god of the fields, germination, strength, courage and love."[5] Professor Roman Zaroff quotes various sources that show the word *jar* or *jari* "has rather ancient roots given that in proto-Indo-European - *jēro/*jōro - has a double meaning, that is, both 'Year' and 'Spring'"[13] while "Yaro" is described as representing "spring, love and looks like Apollo."[44] In Lithuania, the spring feast is called Jores or Trimpos.[45]

In Serbia he is known as Djurdjev and as is said in an Old South Slavic folk song, "...Where Djurdjev walks, there your field gives birth..."[46] In Lithuania he is known as Jore or Joris and is the "God of the Spring Thunder." He owned the "key to the Land," which when it is unlocked it would give forth rain. He "unlocks" the "Gate of Summer" at the beginning of May. Since he is the Lord of Grain they bury bread in the fields and gardens as an offering.

Jarila & Jarilo's Day (St. George's Day/May Day) was recognized as the beginning of the warm half of the year in the earlier herding culture, later the Spring Equinox on March 21st or 22nd took on the rituals of Spring. To add to the confusion, when the "new year" shifted to January 1st instead of the Spring Equinox, some rituals of spring were celebrated on New Year's Day.

In Latvia, he is known as Jumis or Jarun. He is considered a twin with the dark time of year. Any "twinned" fruit or grain is sacred to Jumis, such as two cherries fused together or two heads of wheat on a stalk. You can see Jumis's connection to "Jaro" the beginning of the "year" on May Day. Ancient Slavic depictions show him as a two headed god or with two faces looking both forward and backward. His lore got carried on with Janus, the two-faced God who looks both forward and back in the year. Not only is he crowned with a grain wreath, but he can appear entirely clothed in wheat and barley. He is a healer and rides a white horse, which was carried over with St. George.[47]

What is undoubtedly a sacred spot to this incarnation of the Lord of the Radiant Light and his partner Jarila, is a healing spring at Glava Panega the source of the Zlatna Panega River in Bulgaria. People still go there to seek cures for their illnesses on May Day (St. George's Day.)[48] There is a temple there to the Greek healing god, Asclepius, that is more than two thousand years old.

Jarillo is connected to the cornflower (and probably Jarilla is too, as well as the *rusalka*.) In one Ukrainian tale, a young man with blue eyes was transformed by a *rusalka* into a cornflower. The protective powers of the God and Goddess are held in this flower and it is used to protect mother and child. Cornflowers are harvested on the Summer Solstice and dried to use as broom bristles to make a protective broom that is placed beside the door or fireplace or placed in a child's bedroom. In Bulgaria, one of these sacred brooms is shaped into an effigy of "German" (another name for the god, Jarillo) and used in ritual to stop excessive or violent rain.[49] The Wends (Sorbs) dress a young man at the Summer Solstice as "Jan" or "Johann" in an outfit completely covered in cornflowers to represent the young god.[50] The Komi, a Finno-Ugric tribe of Russia reduced Jarillo to a grain spirit called Peludi-Aika meaning "Father Cornflower" who forbids people from going out on July 20th or their grain would be ruined.

In Belarus, Jarilo is described as "a handsome young man, wearing a white cloak and having on his brow a coronet of flowers. He rode upon a white horse, carrying a sheaf of rye in his left hand, and a human skull in his right hand."[5]

In the Balkans, a festival on May 6th (Jurjevo, St. Juraj's Day, St. George's Day) is celebrated by a girl wearing a skirt of greenery who goes door to door getting water sprinkled on her. She is alternately called a variation of Dodola/Didilya or Perperuna. Here we see the name "Lady Lada" used alternately with Perun's partner, Perperuna. This shows us that Lada & Lado are the young spring form of Perperuna & Perun [see Perunika]. The similarity of the ritual to that of "Green George" and Jarilo, shows that Lada & Lado are the same as Jarilo & Jarila.

Followers: *Călușari, Kalushari, Waydlot* or *Vaidilos*
Sacred Day, Time or Holiday: May Day to Summer Solstice
Sacred Space: bright, open wind-swept hills with water nearby
Sacred Animals: white cock, white horse, snake
Sacred Plants: linden (lime) trees, oaks, wild geraniums (cranesbill geranium), cornflowers, white water lilies, mare's-tail, the legendary blooming fern, ivy, asparagus, willows, hazel trees
Sacred Objects: ribbons, flowers, wedding bells, handfasting ribbon or cloth, phallic symbols and sex

toys (in his warrior aspect a sword and shield), staff, keys (especially a golden key)
Offerings: apples, flower wreaths, honey, gold and golden things, twinned grain head, or twinned fruit, grain, beer, hazelnuts
Symbol: twin horse heads/flails

"The First of May" by unknown artist 1883 as celebrated in England.

"Jerovit" in the Wolgast church by Chron-Paul.

"Coat of arms of Rugāju Municipality, Latvia"
with a twinned head of wheat and three golden
hazelnuts.

Austeja - (OWS-steh-ah) "The Weaver" "The Protective Goddess" "The Joyful Goddess" "The Bee Goddess" (Auseklite, Aesthe, Austė, Austea, Austheia, Austėjaus, Austejos, Austere, Auxteias Vissagīstis, Astuja, Ateya, Ateyas, Inga, Mary-Orans, Orans, Oranta)

Austeja comes from the verb *austi*, meaning "to weave,"[51] since bees were thought to "weave" their honeycombs inside the hive and the Goddess is a weaver of fate. Yet, Austeja's name goes far deeper than that! The Indo-European word *aus* has a dual meaning of "east" and "dawn." This is the direction that we pray to the Radiant Lady of Light. It is probable that the word *austi*, to weave, actually derives from the name of the goddess as she weaves the dawn, as well as all life, into being. The Proto-Indo-European Goddess' name is speculated to be *Aeusos from which comes Austron, the Germanic goddess of dawn and spring. Her name became Eastre/Eostre in Old English, which gives her name to the holiday of Easter.[52] I believe Austeja or Austria was the origin of the country of Austria was named after the Goddess, just as the country of Germany was probably named after Jarillo's name variation of German (or *most* likely from the goddess Germania). Her title of Auxteias Vissagīstis means "giving life to everyone and everything".[53]

The Christian title of "Mary-orans" comes from a gesture of prayer towards the Goddess.

60

SymbolDictionary.net describes the orens position as "It is performed standing, elbows bent or at the side, with arms uplifted and palms upward - a gesture of supplication or pleading."[54] This gesture of the goddess can be seen in Slavic icons of today, in medieval Russian temple rings, through Neolithic goddess sculptures of the Vinca culture, back to sculptures in Çatalhöyük, Turkey dating to 7,400 BCE.

Her origins go back at least 10,000 years. The image of a "bee goddess" has been found carved on bone and cave walls. In Anatolia, Turkey on the other side of the Black Sea from the Slavic lands was found a 10,000 year old statue of a voluptuous Mother Goddess.[55] She has large bee eyes and a "beehive styled tiara" and her body streams with painted lines of golden honey. I'll point out that the nearby island of Rhodes (which was probably named after a variation of the spring goddess Rada) also has the famous Bee Goddess plaque.

It was thought that the bees were messengers to the gods, that the voice of the goddess could be heard in their hum. It was also a Slavic custom to "tell the bees" important news such as a birth or death in the household.[56] Slavs believe that the soul could take the form of a bee, that's why in Russia it was considered sacrilege to kill a bee.[57] To the ancient Slavs the bee was not only a symbol of the soul, but a symbol of friendship and love.

61

Austeja is an especial protector of brides and pregnant women. Marija Gimbutas writes, "Offerings were made to her by jumping while tossing the oblation upward to the ceiling or into the air."[58] Sometimes brides still offer her a libation at their wedding by tossing a toast into the air.

In Celtic lore the bee goddess was transformed to St. Gobnait, whose name means "bringer of joy."[59] One of the reasons the Slavs believed you should not sell your beehive because it would be the equivalent of "selling your own happiness." St. Gobnait protects people and cattle. She is also connected to healing with honey, a bell, white deer and sacred wells at which white deer are said to be seen. Her feast day is February 11th[60] which corresponds with the Bulgarian celebration of the feast of St. Harlampy on February 10th, when beeswax candles and honey are blessed for health and healing purposes. St. Harlampy's name means "glowing with joy," so you can tell these are joyful deities!

We may also get some additional clues as to ancient Slavic traditions from the worship of St. Gobnait that is still practiced today. On February 11th, a two-feet long wooden rough wooden carving (xoanon) of the saint is displayed and ribbons are cut that are the same length as the statue (it may have been a length of wool yarn in the past.) Each person takes a turn processing up to the statue, where you can wind your ribbon around the statue or touch it to "her heart." A different description states that the ribbons are measured along her length and around her width. Supplicants then kiss the statue and the ribbons are taken home and used to protect from illness.[60] This dates back at least to the 13th century in Ireland and looks very similar to the worship of wooden xoanons in the Slavic lands.

Austeje (Orans) is seen with her arms up-stretched towards the skies. She is the goddess of peace, protection, brides, pregnant women, fertility, abundance, joy, sexual pleasure, good health, as well as the provider of delicious food and drink.

Followers: could be *guslarz* or *guslarka* (a musical shamanic practitioner)
Sacred Day, Time or Holiday: February 10th or 11th, May Day Eve and May Day (April 30th, May 1st/6th), August, especially August 2nd and between October 2nd & 10th
Sacred Space: near a beehive, meadows, millpond, streams
Sacred Animals: bees, bull, white deer, dog, ladybugs, butterflies
Sacred Plants: clover, linden tree, heather, meadow flowers, poppy, fruit trees
Sacred Objects: amber, beeswax, figures of bees, anything vulva shaped, chalice, flute, spindle, loom, double-bladed axe, labyrinths

Offerings: mead, *medovukha*, honey-beer, beeswax candle, honey, linden flowers, honeycomb, bread, peas and honey, honey cookies, poppy seeds, bee pollen and royal jelly, fibula (dress pins)
Symbol: the *Auseklas*, the *labrys*, the symbol "Y", and the symbol of Berehynia (like a stylized 6-legged insect)

"Gold plaque of the Bee Goddess" from the Rhodes Acropolis circa 700 BCE photo by Notafly.

"The Virgin Orans" unknown artist, mosaic circa 1000 CE in St. Sophia of Kyiv, Russia.

Auseklis (OWS-see-kleesh) "The God of Life" (Auseklitis, Auśijá, Ausiklitis, Auxtejas Wissagistis, Avsen, Bausen, Deviṇ Ūšiṇe, Dzīvība, Ing, Jūrģis, Jurgis, Kukeri, Mavsen, Tausen, Tavunsiai, Tenis, Tuvsen, *Ośinja, Ousen, Ovsen, Usen, Ūsenis, Ūsinis, Ūsiṇš, Usinsh, Ūzinš) -

The Lithuanians would know him as Ūsiṇš, yet as you can see, the god and goddess pairs each have similar names, so I'll use the title of Auseklis to match his partner. His title of Ovsen means "oats" or pertaining to oats in Serbo-Croation. In the springtime of the year this god is all about pleasure, fertility and "sowing his wild oats"!

Auseklis' name is connected to the Morning Star, the dawn, light, bees and the Hindu gods of light and horses. In Latvian folk songs the name Ūsiṇš is used interchangeably with Jūrģis (George, Jarillo). We know this because May Day (April 23rd in the old Julian calendar and May 6th in the Gregorian calendar) is called both Ūsiṇš Day and Jūrģis Day.[40] Ūsiṇš is the protector of horses and a foal can be his symbol.

The Jesuit priest Joannis Stribingius wrote in 1606, "They [the Latvians] sacrifice to the God of horses, whom they call Deviṇ Ūšiṇe, each two pieces of money and two pieces of bread and a bit of fat which they throw into the fire."[61] An important point is that it is two pieces of money and two pieces of bread are offered to this deity. This shows the connection with the two-faced god Janis and the double-headed wheat or double cherries offered to Jumis (Jore, Jarillo).

In Hindu lore the Asvins are connected to the divine drink of *Soma*, which is equivalent to the ambrosia of Siva (and the Olympian gods) and the honey drink (*medvodka*) of Austeja & Zozim. These produce the "rapturous joy" or inebriated ecstasy that brings about divine revelations and divination. Auseklis joins with his goddess partner and together they increase the fertility of the land with their joyful sex and revelry. Their bells and noise break up the sluggish energy of winter. The ecstatic state brought on by wine, beer or *medvodka* (or cannabis) let their caste of priests and priestesses divine the future year. Ūsiņš particularly protects and cares for horses looking after their wellbeing, as well as the fertility of the fields, the fertility of cows, and the bounty of the bees. He is a fertile, loving, caring, giving god wishing the best for his people.

Followers: *uśíj*
Sacred Day, Time or Holiday: Tuesdays, December 21st (Christmas), New Year's Eve and New Year's Day, February 2nd, 10th, 11th or 14th, March 16th or the Spring Equinox, April 23rd/May 6th, May Day Eve and May Day (April 30th, May 1st/6th), August, especially August 2nd, between October 2nd & 10th and October 27th (the Gate of Winter.)

Sacred Space: near a beehive, meadows, millpond, streams

Sacred Animals: bee, bull, horse (especially a white one), foal, pig

Sacred Plants: clover, linden trees, meadow flowers, poppies, fruit trees, vines, ivy, grapes, chamomile

Sacred Objects: amber, beehive, beeswax, flute, grain

Offerings: (usually offered in pairs) coins, bread and fat (thrown in the fire), honeycomb, beeswax candle, tobacco, alcoholic drinks (especially mead, *medovukha*, and beer), bee pollen, royal jelly, a cock (rooster), eggs, grain, pork

Symbol: the *Ūsiņš* (back to back "E's" with a line or three dots in between) and *auseklis* star.

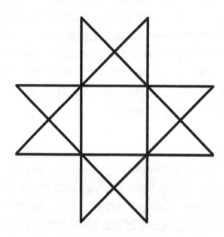

"Sventas Jurgis" in Lithuania, killing the dragon of winter. Photo by Modris Putns.

Devana (Deh-VAH-na) "The Divine One" "The Forest Mother" "The Mother of the Animals" "The Bear Goddess" - (Artia, Dejana, Devana, Diiwica, Dilwica, Diviana, Divona, Gana, JDina, Dzevana, Dzeviana, Dziannica, Dzievanna, Dziewana, Dziewanna, Dziewona, Mamony, Medeina, Svoruna, Zenovia, Zievana, Zievonia, Ziewonia, Ziewanna, Ziewannas, Zvoruna, Zyevanna)

Her name means "Divine" in Hindi, it also means "maiden" in the Slavic languages. While in Lithuanian *duwana* means "gift" or perhaps the "Giving Goddess."[62] Sir James George Frazer tells us that an effigy is carried in from the woods, "which goes by the name of Summer, May, or the Bride: in the Polish districts it is called Dziewanna, the goddess of spring."[63] She has been called a virgin, but she is also the Mother of the Animals. She is a "mistress" in the manner in which we use the honorific "Ms." Fierce and strong, nimble and crafty, brave and proud, the goddess Devana roams the woods of the Carpathian mountains and beyond. She managed to hold her own with the warrior culture, who saw her combined with the swiftness of the mare and armed with bow and arrows. Yet her worship existed before the last Ice Age, before horses were ever domesticated. In Poland she is sometimes called Vesna Devana where she trades places with Morana/Marzanna, the Dark Goddess.[64]

70

Her name in Lithuania is Žvorunė-Medina:[65] Medina or Medeina meaning the "Forest Goddess," Žvorunė or Zvoruna, the "Beast Goddess," or Vilkmerge, the "Girl of Wolves."[66] While Devana is said to be able to transform into any animal, she usually appears as a bear or a wolf. She keeps her hair unbound, wild and free and like her Slavic witches go into the woods to work magic with their hair unbound. In her human form she wears a bearskin and is sometimes depicted with two wolf companions. The constellation of The Great Mother Bear is her reflected in the night sky.

In Celtic lore, the Bear Goddess is called Artia based on the Proto-Indo-European word for "bear." It is from this PIE root that we get the words for "arctic" and "art"[67] but they stopped using the PIE word because saying the name of the bear was taboo. Instead they used Devana, The Divine One. This shows that Devana/Artia is the common origin of both the Greek Artemis and Roman Diana and her radiant brother/lover got turned into Apollo. While some classists have suggested that the Roman goddess Diana may have been the origin of Devana, with a pre-proto-Indo-European origin to her name that dates to *at least* before 4,000 BCE, while the Greek culture started around 2,000 BCE. However, I believe her worship goes back even further.

Mugwort is sacred to the Bear Goddess. It's Latin name, *Artemisia vulgaris*, shows it is sacred to

Artemis. The tea, elixir or smoke helps with prophetic dreams and divination.[68] (The word "divination", "divine" and Devana come from the same PIE root.) [69]

In Korea, moxibustion is a treatment of burning mugwort on points of the body for healing. Its invention is credited to their god-emperor, Dangun but it turns out that Dangun is the son of the "bear-woman," Ungnyeo, who prayed under a sacred birch tree and was granted a son.[70] (The birch also being sacred to Devana.) It sounds to me like the male-centric Korean culture didn't want to give the credit to the Bear Goddess!

The name *dziewanna* or *devana* is given to the mullein plant.[71] Not only does mullein have healing powers, and the smoke aids in psychic visioning, the dried woody stalks are very flammable and were used to make candle wicks. These candles were blessed on February 2nd, known today as Candlemas Day. The goddess Devana was transformed in Christian Orthodox lore as "Our Lady of the Thunder Candle" or "Fiery Mary" whose feast day was February 2nd. As "Our Lady of the Thunder Candle" she protects people from the wolves, but she *also* tells the wolves what they are allowed to eat. She is the keeper of the balance of life.

The Cross Quarter day of February 2nd is Bear Day, a day when a bear looks out from hibernation and if he sees his shadow there is six more weeks of winter. As you might have guessed, this is the origin of Groundhog Day.[72] This is one of the dates that the worship of Devana in her winter form (along with her partner Veles) then begins to change into their spring form.

Once she was seen as the same as Žyva (Siva), the Bird Goddess but their worship diverged. I suspected this because their attributes were much the same but two facts confirm this. First, in Slovenia mugwort is called *Vidinia zel* meaning "Vida's herb"[73] (Vida being a variation of Siva.) Second, the first written sentence in human history is "The Bear Goddess is the Bird Goddess is the Bear Goddess, indeed!" This was found on a 6,000 year old spindle whorl from the region around the Danube river and was translated from the Vinca script by Toby Griffin.[74]

Followers: *dziwożony, biserka or bosorka, calusari*
Sacred Day, Time or Holiday: Mondays, February 2nd, May Day Eve and May Day, June 21st (Summer Solstice,) August 15th, October 21st (or 26th or 31st)
Sacred Space: forests, wooded mountains, rivers, lakes, elm grove, moonlit clearings in the woods, crossroads
Sacred Animals: bear, marten, weasel, fox, wolf, mare, hare
Sacred Plants: mullein (*devana*), elm, rowen, mugwort, St. John's Wort, toothwort, dragonswort,

wolfsbane, wormwood, basil, birch, elm, evergreen, pine, spruce
Sacred Objects: silver, moonstone, natural stone, drinking horn, amber, Spondylus shells
Offerings: venison, a hare, red wine, carved animals, incense made from dried mullein, mead, fruits, amber stones or amber incense, beads, necklaces and amulets made from Spondylus shells

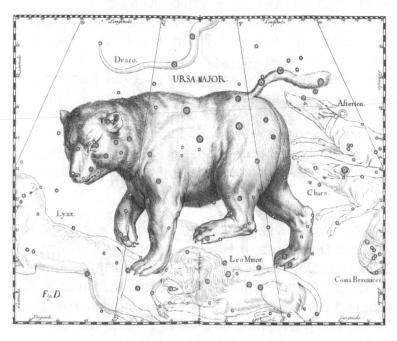

"Ursa Major" by Johannis Hevelii 1690.

"Artio - The Bear Goddess" in the Mythology of All
Races by Louis H. Gray. 1918.

"Diana" by Cherubino Alberti circa 1580.

Dazbog (DASH-boog) "The Giving God", "The God of Good Fortune," "The Lord of Life Giving Radiance"- (Dabog, Daboga, Dadźbóg, Dagebog, Dai-bog, Dajbog, Dajbogec, Dassuba, Dasuba, Dasuva, Dasva, Dasyebog, Daybog, Dažb, Dažbog, Dazboga, Dažboh-Čors, Daždbog, Dazhb, Dazhbog, Dazh-bog, Dazhboga, Dazhdbog, Dazhboga, Dazhdzhbog, Dazibogu, Hors Dazbog, Khors Dazbog, Pel wihkse, Pilwitos, Szkahde, Xors Dazbog)

Dazbog's name is considered by several Slavic experts to come from the Proto-Indo European verb *dati, meaning "to give," thus he is the "Giving-God."[75] At his essence, Dazbog is abundance and fertility and gives us all good things. In Lithuania, his name means good fortune and he is paired with the goddess of fortune, Dola (who is also known as Lada). He has been called "Dazhdbog the Kind." In the neglected realm of Slavic studies the country of Belarus is often overlooked. While some countries have forgotten that Dazbog had a goddess partner, in Belarus, they record that he has Zyva as his mother, marries the Goddess of Spring Lada-Liola and they are recorded as having a son Jaryla.[5]   So let's untangle this...

Looking at the god and goddess partnerships of Siva and Seibog, Vit and Vita, the spring couples of Lada and Lado who are the same as Jarila and Jarilo, the logical connection is that Dazbog would have been paired with Dziva (Siva), as the life-giving sun energy partnered with the water and rain goddess. We find that the names Dola and Dodola are alternately used for that of Lada. The Russians came up with an explanation stating that Dazbog was married three times: to Maja Zlatogorka (meaning Golden Hill), Marena, and Zhiva (Siva). This shows the triple goddess through the wheel of the year: Summer, Winter and Spring. In these tales, Dazbog has three helping "power animals": a snake, a wolf and an eagle/falcon named Rarog.[44] The snake would represent the Underworld, the wolf represents the Middle World and the eagle/falcon for the Upper World.

Through the ages, Dziva (Siva), the Goddess of Living Water is eclipsed, so that her name is not even recognized as being the origin of the word rain and the god is credited with it. Aleksandra Kojic states, "One of his names is Daždbog and *"dažd"* in many Slovenian languages (Slovak, Czech, Russian, and Polish) means rain."[76] In keeping with this combined role, in Belarus "Dazhdzhbog" is the god of rain and sun and consequently worshipped as an agricultural god. Large glacial stones that are sacred to him have a depression or hollow in them in which sacred grain was ground to make sacrificial bread.

Radosavljevich states that the 12th century writings of the monk Nestor tell us, "The god of fire was Dabog or Dai-bog (the god of sun and sunshine, the giver of life and of all good things, the god of prosperity, light and every progress)…"[77] William Ralston describes him as "Dazhbog, the Day-God."[6] He is reputed to ride a white horse. Dazbog would seem to have assimilated the powers of his female partner.

In Slovenia we see "Dajbogec," the diminutive of Dajbog, invoked in early spring (which would make Dajbogec another name for Jarilo/Lado.) Boris Čok describes a ritual to "Dajbogec" which took place on the hill, Pri belem Krizu. "There was a stone circle, divided into four parts, with a stone slab in each of them. The girls performed a special ritual with a braid of ivy, soaked in the water of the magic spring Vroce (Vrocek). In a ritual song, they prayed to 'Dajbogec' for warmth, fertility of crops and 'sun in the sky.' Meanwhile, men lit a bonfire on the top of the hill and prayed for a rich harvest by throwing a fruit into the fire."[78]

Yet it looks like Dazbog has a seasonal component to his powers since we find Dazbog looking like an old man in Serbian lore. This can cause some researchers like Nikos Čausidis to assert that there are "two Dazbogs: an Eastern-Slavic, Solar Dazbog and the chthonic deity of the South Slavs,"[79] when it is really just two different "masks" of this seasonal deity. In Serbia Dazbog is connected to the "black" role of the sun in the winter, and is called the "Shepherd of Wolves."[80] In Dazbog's elderly form he is sometimes referred to as "Hromi Daba" which means "Lame Daba" which classically trained scholars connect with Hephaistos, the lame smith of the underworld. So we can tell from the Greek lore and Dazbog's connection with the chthonic world during winter, that Dazbog became a god of blacksmiths upon the discovery of shaping iron (between 2,000 and 1,000 BCE.)[81]

Dazbog's fertile, creative energy makes him a patron of metallurgy, blacksmiths, artisans, and other craft people. He is often depicted as a lame old man wrapped in a dark bearskin with wolves as his companions. Sometimes he is missing an eye.[76] (Having only one eye meant you could see into the spirit world, which is why Odin is said to have one eye and why Vulcan is described as having cyclops who worked for him.) To differentiate between Dazbog's summer and winter qualities his elderly winter form can be referred to as Hors-Dazbog, Khors-Dazbog, or Xors-Dazbog.

Sacred Day, Time or Holiday: January 14th, Solstices and Equinoxes
Sacred Space: hills and mountains
Sacred Animals: white horse, wolf, boar, snake, eagle or falcon
Sacred Plants: grains
Sacred Objects: anvil, blacksmithing tools, sun symbols, metal ore, boar tusk, stone with a hollow
Offerings: candle, bread, coal, gold, silver, gemstones, water from a blacksmith's forge, rain

water, Jägermeister liqueur (which means Forest Master)

"De smidse van de cyclopen" (The Forge of the Cyclops) by Cornelis Cort 1572.

81

By this point you should be able to see enough
similarities, and even cross-overs of titles to see that
these were essentially the same deities that just
developed slightly differently in different areas of Old
Europe. If you are familiar with Celtic lore, you may
begin to notice that the beliefs are essentially the
same. A fact that becomes even more obvious when
you know about the holidays and magic. However,
as practitioners of magic know, belief creates reality.
So each of these Goddesses or Gods offer us a
slightly different way to connect with the immensity of
the Divine All.

From Münster's Sights & Views
Flying snake of winter captured by a stork of summer.

SUMMER

Siva (SEE-vah) "Life Goddess", "The Goddess", "The Radiant Goddess of Life-Giving Water", "The Bird Goddess" or "The Mother of Life" (Ciotia, Dael, Deva, Diva, Divača, Dziva, Kaliada, Laima, Razivia, Siwa, Vida, Vita, Žemina, Zhiva, Zhywie, Živa, Ziza, Zmiya, Žyva, Zywie, Zywye) -

Siva means "living, being, existing." She literally means "life." While Diva is based on the ancient Slavic *divъ*, which means "shiny, heavenly or divine," which shows up in the Sanskrit word *diva*.[82] She is the divine Bird Goddess.

Polish scholar, Dagmara Dziekan, explains, "*żywić* means also to nourish, feed, cherish; and the noun *żywicielka* could describe a provider, breadwinner or a feeding mother."[83] While the name Ziva in Sanskrit means "the one who is kind."[84] Probably the earliest form of her name is Ziza which has the onomatopoeia of bees buzzing. (Since I believe the very earliest words were simply imitations of the sounds of the natural world and she is an ancient, ancient goddess.) The divine couple of Austeja and Auseklas are another way to approach the goddess Siva and her partner Seibog, specifically in their role of joyful fertility deities and providers of sweet abundance. If we needed any more confirmation that the Bear Goddess, Devana is essentially the same as the Bird Goddess, Siva, of which the Bee Goddess,

Austeja is just another "face", we can see where
Artemis (the Greek form of Devana/Artia) has
priestesses called *Melissaonomoi*, meaning
"beekkeepers." We also have Demeter, Rhea and
Cybele's priestesses who are called *Melissai* or
Melissae meaning "bees."[56]

Siva is the goddess of the energy of life, eternal love,
partnership, friendship and the cycle of life. In
Slovakia, she is known as Diva which translates there
to "maiden." In Slovenia, she is known as Živa,
Nikrmana, Velika Mat', meaning the "Great Mother"
or Velika Baba, the "Great Crone." So she can be
seen in all her permutations of Maiden, Mother and
Crone. Her partner is the god, Siebog/Devač.

In Latvia, she is known as Deivė Laima. Laime
means "happiness or "luck,"[36] so she is the
Goddess of Joy and Good Fortune. Siva is also the
goddess of justice starting with the natural rules of
life itself; such as if you pollute your water you will get
sick or if you over-harvest a plant you won't have its
medicine anymore.

In various descriptions she is described as nude with
cascading golden hair down to her knees, crowned
with roses or ripe wheat, holding an apple and
grapes. (Notice how that is basically the same as the
description of Jarila and Vesna.) The Romans called
her Venus and she was their "**Lady Luck**".[85] Her

sacred day is Friday (starting from the evening of Thursday night and running to Friday at sunset.)

In a rare description from 1710 of the Pagan beliefs of Moravia, M. Stredowsky describes "Siwa." He writes:
"This goddess had a temple at Brin, which has been turned into a church. The author says it was a stately building, gold and precious stones shined in it on all sides. Siwa, the Goddess of Love, appeared naked, under the figure of a young maid of an ordinary size. The hair of that deity hung down to her knees. Her crown was made of roses and boughs of myrtle-tree. A rose came out of her mouth, and a bright ray out of her heart, and one might see the heart of the goddess through a hole made for that purpose. In one of her hands she had a globe representing the world, and in the other, three golden apples. She was seated upon a gold chariot, drawn by two swans, and two white pigeons. The three graces, naked as she was, attended upon her, and turning their backs gave golden apples to one another."[22]

In Belarus she was described as a beautiful fertility goddess "wearing on her head a crown of ripe ears of wheat, and bearing fruits in her hands. She was filled with kindness and compassion towards mankind."[5]

She can transform into a cuckoo who flies to the spirit world and brings back news of one's fate. Her symbol in Latvia is ">>>lll<<<" and this would seem to go back 8,000 years to the ancient Vinca culture, where sculptures of the Bird Goddess are marked with three parallel lines, and/or chevrons (the "V" shape.) The constellation of Cygnus the Swan is her's and brings the deceased souls back to her via the Milky Way (also called the Bird Way or the Fairy Way.) She also has a connection to the "Morning Star" (the planet Venus).[86]

She heals with her "living water" and her followers are healers as well, called "white women" connected to the shining white *vila* and watery *rusalka* (the fey.) She is connected to all the birds, but especially white ones like doves, ducks and swans. In some parts of Russia the swan is looked upon as a bird which ought not to be shot at and is connected to the fairies, the white *vilas* and the water *rusalkas*.[87] In one tale, the *vila* guard a fountain and can change into swans. This would also seem to connect this fountain to the "White Goddess" since they are her servants. The goddess in her form as a duck, created the earth we live on by diving deep into the water and bringing up the dirt in her bill to her divine partner. (This story morphed into a tale of the Slavic gods Veles and Perun, and eventually the Devil and God.) Her's is also the chamois goat with golden horns.

Siva would also seem to be connected to the white snake. Zmago Šmitek writes "the white snake is the mother of all other snakes, and she can be summoned by playing the flute and reading 'black [magic] books." He cites Tušek's work recording the Upper Carniolan tradition that whoever "licks a white snake, becomes all-knowing."[87] [Carniola is an area rich in the lore of Siva/Diva.] There are many examples of snakes conveying the ability to understand the "language of the birds" or the "language of the plants" and knowing the plant uses and even conveying the power of prophecy. Šmitek goes on to convey that the white snake has the ability to fly through the air. In this it is very like the image of the winged serpent or dragon, they both make a sort of whistling noise and sometimes the dragon too can grant the ability to understand the "language of the birds."[87] Licking or eating the snake (or dragon heart, or the jewel in the snake's head) should be understood in a shamanic capacity of incorporating that energy of the goddess into yourself in order to gain wisdom.

Siva spins and shapes the energy of life and teaches her devotees how to do it as well. Siva is the Great Goddess. She heals by harnessing the energy of life and imbuing it into her living waters. Siva is the patron of seers and healers, known as "white women." August Dimitz references Valv. (VII 476) stating, "The country people of his time recognized and venerated as higher beings (*Boginje*) the white women, who had secret knowledge of the healing powers of herbs, pointed out stolen property, etc. and thus represented the principle of goodness in opposition to the witches."[88] (By this point "witches" were demonized by the church, yet people still recognized the good, healing power embodied in the "white women." The Celts also use the same term. In Latvia, her name of Lauma is used for the word for witches.) A *vila* in Serbia can also called "white lady" or "white woman"[19] and to them also are attributed healing and foretelling powers. It is also believed that a magic worker or "white woman" may have a *vila* back in their family tree. Like the goddess, many Slavic magic workers go out in the woods and do their spell-work naked. Siva is Queen of the *Vile* (Fairies). They do her bidding and help teach her devotees. The *vile* are also described as "white women."

She is love, since that is what brings people together. Her sacrament is joyful, loving sex. Siva is the force that spins the life energy into the child in the womb, or pushes up the flowers and grain. She is the creative force that continues through us when we sing, dance, draw, play, paint, or program!

She still continues that creativity today as the original Mother Goose, with her Pagan teaching tales hidden in "fairy tales".

Followers: *kazlary*, "white women" *bela zena* In Latvia and Lithuania, a male priest of hers is the *Menuo* and a female priestess is *Menesis Menulis. Mildawnikas, Samovila or Boginje*

Sacred Day, Time or Holiday: Fridays, May Day (May 6th,) May 13th, May 27th or the last Sunday in May, *Rusaliia* in June, also August 1 or 2

Sacred Space: islands or near springs, rivers, and lakes

Sacred Animals: cuckoo, sow, cows, does, bees, ducks, geese, swans, pigeons, doves, snakes, goats (mountain ibex or *steinbok*), especially white ones

Sacred Plants: Linden tree (especially one with three trunks), fruitful plants (especially apples and grapes), birch, willow, mugwort

Sacred Objects: birch wreath, chalice, bell, ocarina (*sistulka*), flute, *gemshorn* (flute made from chamois goat horn), pan pipes, golden amber, drinking horn, bird amulets, yarn, wool, flax, spindle, the rainbow, stars/ the planet Venus, the constellation Cygnus

Offerings: golden apples, grapes, fruit, honey, a lump of beeswax as incense, horns, chamois leather, amber, embroidered towels (*rushnik*), feathers

Symbol: >>>III<<< or just the "V"

"Siwa" from Westphalen's book print, 1740.

"Siwa" by Andrej S. Kajsarov. 1804.

OLD

MOTHER GOOSE
And the Golden Egg.

OLD Mother Goose,
 When she wanted to wander,
Would ride through the air,
 On a very fine gander.

"Old Mother Goose and the Golden Egg" circa 1860.

Siebog (SEE-boog) "Life God", "The Young Lord of Life-Giving Radiance" (Crodo, Crodos, Deiws, Devač, Devačo, Devar, Devin, Deywis, Dievaitis, Dievas, Dievs, Diviriks, Dovač, Gibog, Jibog, Krodos, Sibog, Zhibog) -

As the pure, divine couple, they are brother and sister, lovers and partners in creation. He is the radiant god of love, fertility and partnership, equally as important as his sister/partner/mate, Siva. As she is the embodiment of the blossoming of the life force, he is the spark that triggers it. Together they encapsulate the duality of regeneration and the magic of life. Devar in Hindi means, "King of the Gods," (as well as Devī being their "Great Mother Goddess.")[89] In the Baltics, Dievs, just literally means "God." He eventually became better known under the name of Svarog or Dabog. Dažbog's name literally means "giver of life" and he is associated with the life-giving power of sunshine as well as incorporating the goddess' nurturing rain.

Remember, Siebog is not "The Sun," the sun was known as the female Saule or Solntse. The same goes for the Celtic religion where the sun was known by the female names of Sulis.[90] Siebog is the "Radiant Lord." Siebog is shining energy in any form. Like the Celtic springtime god Bel (or Belenus, meaning "Bright One") a radiant god associated with the life-giving power of fire and the sunlight. His partner is Belisama, meaning "the brightest one," or

(interestingly enough) "the most powerful."[91]
Belisama is a goddess of healing and of water just
like the fair, "glowing" Siva/Diva. Also, just like Siva's
special day of May 6th, these Celtic deities also
celebrated their time of revelry on Beltane, May 6th
(now commonly celebrated May 1st.) The classically
educated monks familiar with Roman deities
connected Belisama to Minerva, but never thought to
look to the Slavic goddesses, which provide a *much*
better match.

Siebog is shiningly fair with blond hair since he
represents the shining life-bringing energy that comes
from the sun and fire. The fire in the home was seen
as the Radiant Lord's presence and it was treated
with respect. In his role as the Lord of the Life-Giving
Light, he is connected to the deer, specifically the
white stag, sometimes depicted with golden antlers.
This possibly connects to the Babylonian celestial
stag which is also associated with the sun and fire.
Researcher Malisa Reshke writes, "His antlers
represent rays of sunlight and the annual regrowth
symbolizes the rebirth of the sun after the winter
solstice."[92] Dawn was a special time for this god
and Pagans ritually greeted the sun. Researcher
Marija Gimbutas writes of an Arab traveler and
chronicler, Al-Mas'udi from the 10th century. He
recorded that the Slavs had a temple with an opening
in a dome to let in the sunlight. He also wrote that
they incorporated into the architecture a way to

observe the sunrise.[93] Although often just an open spot on a hilltop is used as Seibog's sacred space.

Seibog is a lover and connected with phallic symbols and grain. He is a kind, protective, nurturing deity. He provides food in the form of plentiful herds and bountiful crops.   As lord of the grain and of joy, Seibog is connected with beer making as well.[94] The Indo-European roots of words give us a clue that Siva's apples were probably used to prepare a fermented ritual drink that let one get in touch with Siva and Seibog and their creativity.

Sacred Day, Time or Holiday: Sunrises, Solstices and Equinoxes
Sacred Space: hills near springs or lakes
Sacred Animals: bear, boar, white stag, white goat (specifically the alpine ibex a/k/a *steinbock*), ox or bull, rooster, hare/rabbit
Sacred Plants: the seeds of fruitful plants, mustard flowers, Silphium (Laserwort)
Sacred Objects: goat horn (particularly chamois goat), bull's horn, ram's horn, drinking horn, bell, rod with ivy, stalactites, phallic shapes, sun-wheel, fire
Offerings: seeds, phallic objects, green (for fertility), white, chamois leather, yellow flowers, sunflowers, candle, golden amber, white or golden horse figurine, basket of seeds, coins, rings, precious stones
Symbol: Sun wheel

"Crodos" by Andrej S. Kajsarov 1804 (one of the
names of Seibog).

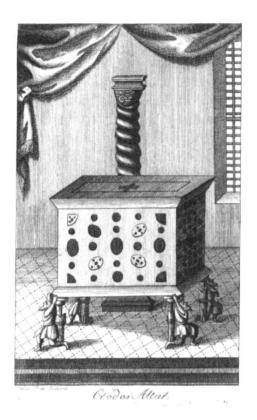

Crodos Altar.

"Crodos Altar" by Andrej S. Kajsarov from the
Versuch diner Slavischen Mythology 1804 This 12th
century altar is made entirely of bronze and is housed
in the Goslarer Museum in Goslar, Germany.

Perunika (PEH-roon-ick-ah) "The Great Mother" "The Goddess of Living Water" (Babarudă, Băbărugă, Babatuţă, Buduroasă-roasă, Didilela, Dodol, Dodola, Dodole, Dudula, Dzidzileyla, Dzidzilia, Dzidzililya, Grmuša, Mătăhulă, Ognyena Maria, Paparuda, Paparugă, Peperuna, Percuna, Percunatele, Pereplut, Perkuna, Perkunatele, Perkunateli, Perkūnė, Perkūnėlė, Perperuna, Piorunka, Pirpiruna, Preperuda, Pripegala, Zezylia, Zizilia and Zyzylas) -

Perun is the god of thunder and Perunika, the goddess of lightning and rain. We see variations of this name in the Balkans, where it is connected to a ritual conducted on May 6th, where a young girl dressed in a skirt of greenery goes around to the different houses and gets sprinkled (our doused) with water. This seems to be just a variation of the ritual where the young spring god (Jarilo/Lado) gets sprinkled with water or dunked on May 6th. There are many variations of this ritual involving a nude young girl (sometimes a boy) dressed in flowers or greenery whirling, dancing and getting doused with water. In some places they lost the knowledge of its rain-inducing powers and it just became a holiday celebrated on the Summer Solstice.

Linguist Stephen Rudy states, "In some areas of Serbia and Bulgaria the name Perperuna is replaced by Dodola or Dudula, and a similar form *du (n) dulis* (tied with an onomatopoeic verb for thunder) is currently substituted by Lithuanians for the tabued Perkunas."[95] The names Didilela, Didilia, Didilya, Doda, Dodol, Dodola, Dodole, Dodoliţă, Dodoloaie, Dudula, Duduleţu, Dudulya, Dudylya, Dzidzileyla, Dzidzilia, Dzidzililya, Zezylia, Zizilia and Zyzylas are most accurately translated as "Lady Lada" or "Great Lada" and compared to "Venus" goddess of love, yet these are are often used as another name for Perunika. These may be viewed as more of her springtime incarnation. Her name variation of Peperouda has come to mean "Butterfly." [96] In Roumania, it also means "poppy." This is because the goddess and the soul can transform into a butterfly and the trance inducing poppy is used to connect with the goddess and her foretelling powers. But originally, these are onomatopoeic names meant to sound like the dripping rain, just as some of Perun's names sound like thunder. Perunika's connection to Siva is clear, since one of Siva's alternative names is Gromowka, the "Queen of Lightning."[4] While in Lithuania, "Perkunatele" has been called the "Queen of Heaven" and was depicted arising from clouds with a scepter in her hand.[36]

February 2nd is a celebration of Perun's partner, Perunika, essentially merged with that of Devana or Vesna as well. It is still celebrated in Poland and other countries, under the worship of "Lady Maria Percunatele," "the Very Holy Mary of the Thunder," or "Our Lady of the Thunder Candles."[6] Candles are lit and blessed, then extinguished and taken home.

99

When severe storms impend, they are lit in front of their home icon.

In a Serbian song, Elijah gets the holy thunder of heaven, but Fiery Mary gets the arrows and lighting. [97] Her's is also the rainbow. In Samarina, Greece, this goddess is certainly connected with water as the phrase, *"Mi adrai Piripruna dip,"* "I became a regular Pirpiruna," is a slang phrase for "I got soaked!"[98]

Followers: *Dodole, Paparuda, Pirpiruna, Preperuša, Preperuša*
Sacred Day, Time or Holiday: July 20 or 22 or Lammas (August 2nd)
Sacred Space: mountains and hilltops
Sacred Animals: snakes, ladybugs, butterflies
Sacred Plants: ash trees, iris flowers, poppies
Sacred Objects: ropes, string,
Offerings: eggs (especially from a black hen,) milk (especially from a black cow or goat,) bread, honey, apples, rainbow colored ribbons
Symbol: rosette

"Paparuda" drawn by Frédéric de Haenen from a
sketch by Rook Carnegie - 1905.

"The Fiery Chariot of the Word" - 19th century icon of
Ognyena Maria with her symbol of the rosette.

Perun (PEH-roon) "The Lightning/Thunder God" "The God of the Oak" "The Fiery One" "The Roaring One" - (Bruzgulis, Diviriks, Divirkis, Dewas Perkunas, Dudulis, Dundulis, Fercun, Grom, Gromovnik, Grumutis, Karevit, Karewit, Keraunos, Parcuns, Pargu, Parjanya, Parkuns, Parom, Pärun, Pehrkun, Peraunos, Percuno, Perein, Perenda, Perëndi, Pergene, Pergrubris, Pergrubrius, Periani, Perndi, Peron, Perone, Peroon, Peruns, Perunu, Perkhons, Perkonas, Perkun, Perkuno, Perkunos, *Perkwunos, Perunas, Peruničić, Perunovski, Perusan, Perusice, Peryun, Petuno, Pjarun, Piarun, Piorun, Pirgene-Pas, Pirwa, Pirwe, Porguini, Pornev, Porun, Prave, Pravy, Prohn, Prone, Prones, Prono, Pronote, Prove, Proven, Provo, Prown, Prun, Porenutius, Puran, Purginepas, Pur'ginepaz, Pyerun, Rhugevit, Rinvit, Riuvit, Ruevit, Rugiavit, Rugievit, Rugiewit, Rujevit, Termes, Tiermas, Ukko, Vanajumal)

Perun is connected to the lightning and thunder. Perun's name derives from the Indo-European root, *perk, perg* or *per*, meaning "to strike" as in the strike of a lightning bolt.[99] H. Munro Chadwick cites the linguistic connection between the Indo-European word *perkuus* to the Latin *quercus* meaning "oak", speculating that Perun means "The God of the Oak". [100] Znayenko identifies *perun* as the word for "thunder" used by the warrior horsemen, the Sarmatians,[101] which would account for Perun's very war-like character. In Polish, the word for lightning is *piorun*. In Russia they use the word *perun* for fire.[23] *Grom* is an onomatopoeic word for "thunder" and *perti* means "to strike."[102] In Slovenia, he is called Gromovnik (The Thunder God). [19]

In Belarus, "Piarun" is pictured as a "tall well-built man with black hair and long golden beard." In other depictions his hair is silver or he is depicted without a beard and described with mustaches only. In other descriptions he has flaming red hair. In one hand, he holds his arrows of lightning and in the other hand, a bow or a rainbow.

Professor Roman Zaroff points out the similarities between Perun and the Indian weather god, Parjanya pointing to an Indo-European origin[103] which then seems to have traveled along with the Thracians. [104] Zaroff points out the similarities between Perun, the Celtic Taranis, the Germanic Thor/Donar and the Greek Zeus. He also writes, "the concept of a Perun-like deity was common amongst the Old European population of Eastern Europe in the middle of the second millennium BCE."[99] Perun's name as "Perkunas" may be the oldest variation of the Thunder God, so if he was the origin of the Greek god Zeus, that would push Perun's worship back even further. Mount Lykaion in ancient Greece is the oldest known site of Zeus's worship dating back to 1,500 BCE, yet there is evidence of prior worship there dating back to 3,000 BCE, probably to a "sky and weather god" on the mountain peak.[105] With the Proto-Indo-European word origin that pushes our date back to 4,500 BCE. William Tooke speculates that Perun was perhaps the same deity whom the ancient Scythians revered under the name of Popeus. [106] In Latvia, the "thunder god" is called Vanajumal which could connect to the Hindu Vajradhara or Vajrabhrt.

The authors Yoffe & Krafczik state the "Greek *keraunos*, a name or epithet of the thunder god, and also meaning thunderbolt, is probably an alteration for a tabooed *Peraunos, a name for the thunder god." They also state that the Greek noun *korune* is a wooden staff or club.[107] Yet considering all the variations of the name of Perun, it seems to me that the Greeks may have been using his true name of Keraunos, since the Greeks were more casual in their use of the sacred names.

The Prussian Priest, Simon Grunau, wrote in the 1500's that Perkun, Patollo and Potrimpo were believed to inhabit the sacred oak grove at Romove. "Perkuno" communed with the priests there in thunderstorms. In his honour a perpetual fire was kept burning under the oak. According to Grunau "Perun's likeness, as depicted on King Widowuto's banner [in the 6th century], was that of a middle-aged man with black beard and wrathful expression of countenance; his head was crowned with flames."[100]

In a rare description from 1710 about the Pagan beliefs of Moravia it states, "The god Peron [sic] was represented standing, armed, with a crown on his head. His ears were like those of an ass. He held a broad iron, like a plow-share, in his right hand, and a standard in the left. His temple was in a wood. Those who pretended to be innocent of the crimes charged upon them, were carried to that temple, and obliged to prove their innocence, by touching the iron that was in the hand of the god, after it had been made red-hot. This sort of trial continued among the Moravians when they had embraced Christianity, till the reign of the Emperor Charles IV."[22] While this was the first time I ever heard Perun was depicted with "ass's ears" I do know that method of "trial by fire" was a common one. It was believed that if a person could escape this relatively unscathed, the god favored them, and if the person touched the hot iron and got huge blisters or died of an infection that was the god's judgement against them.

He is sometimes described as riding a "two-wheeled cart harnessed by two goats..."[108] Both Thor and Perun share the same sacred day of the week, which the Baltic Slavs called "Perendan" (Perun's Day,)[109] but we call Thursday (Thor's Day.) Perun, like his Norse counterpart, carried a huge stone hammer that would return to his hand when he threw it. So many people state that Perun is "like Thor," but it has been speculated that if Perun's hammer was made of stone, and Thor's hammer was made of iron, wouldn't Perun be the original deity on whom Thor is modeled? Also Perun's name goes back to the oldest Proto-Indo-European root, whereas Thor comes from the Proto-German which is derived from Proto-Indo-European. Eventually in the Iron Age, Perun would also be symbolized by his sacred axe. His axe is used to split the clouds and make it rain. However, it may be that his earliest depictions were with a club.

In most sources you will see Perun and Veles at eternal war with each other, stealing each other's wife and cattle throughout the year. However, the earlier Pagan view was much more of a circular dance. In the older Slavic view of the cyclical turning of nature, Perun the sky god takes his turn with Veles the Lord of the Underworld in their dominance over nature. The natural progression of day and night, awake and dreaming would describe them better. Both are needed for balance. Perun is represented in the logical, methodical, conscious world and Veles is the realm of the intuitive, creative, unconscious. Veles and Perun are like the left brain and the right brain working together. They trade places throughout the year; with the active, working, sunny spring and summer and the darkening autumn and winter when food is gathered and our thoughts begin to turn inward. One of the dates where they intersect is February 2nd, sometimes called St. Vasily's Day (for Veles) while modern Rodnovers consider it one of Perun's Days.

The Zoastronists and Christians converted this to their idea of duality, good and bad, heaven and hell. Perun being the sky god got put in Heaven and Veles' Watery Underworld was transformed into Hell. I have to emphasize, there is more of a balance between Perun and Veles. Perun and Veles are the cycle of Light and Darkness increasing and decreasing throughout the year. Perun is pictured with a fiery chariot. Veles lives in the dark of the winter and is lord of death. Veles is vanquished in the Spring and then is honored with the final harvest of the year. When the spring "new year" changed to be the same date as the Winter Solstice, their "changing of the guard" got shifted to those dates. So you will see it both spring to fall or Winter Solstice to Summer Solstice.

Followers: *waidlotten* or *waidelotte* and the high priest was the *kirwaito* or *Kreve (Koive)* or *Greve*
Sacred Day, Time or Holiday: Thursdays, Summer Solstice & August 2nd
Sacred Space: wooded hills, mountains and hilltops
Sacred Animals: anything with black fur or feathers, ravens, eagles, oxen or beasts of burden, red rooster
Sacred Plants: mushrooms, iris (called *perunika*), hazel, hawthorn, rowan, mistletoe, oaks, bladdernut, golden apples, horehound, Royal Fern
Sacred Objects: neolithic stone points, thunder stones (belamites), golden key, garnets, rubies,

carbuncles, amber, whip of iron wire, whip of tin,
quartz, quartzite, fire-making flints, iron fire-striker

"The Prince Vladimir in 980 [CE] makes orders at an
idol of Peruna." A miniature from the Radziwiłł
Chronicle illuminated manuscript from the 15th
Century.

A bronze amulet of Perun from the 12th Century.
This seems to be a common stance for Perun in
medieval amulets.

Vit (VEET) "Lord" or Svantovit (svant-oh-VEET) "The Radiant Lord" "The Holy Lord"((Beli, Byali, Suantevit, Sutvid, Suvid, Svantevid, Svantovitus, Svarozhits, Svaty, Sventovit, Svet, Svetovid, Sviantovit, Sviatovid, Sviatoy Vit, Svyentovit, Swanto-vit, Swarag, Swiatowit, Syetovit, Veit, Vid, Vide, Vitus, Wit, Witislaw, Zuantevith, Zuantewith, Zvantewith)

In Serbia, the Summer Solstice is called *Vidovdan*, the day of *Sveti Vid* (Svetovid.) Showing a variation of this deity's name, Vid or Vit (meaning power, strength, energy.) *Sveti* means "light" or "shining," which means he is the "Shining Lord of Energy." (To further confuse things the word *sveti* also became the word for saint, so he was also called Saint Vit or Vitus. This is why saints are depicted with a halo of light around their head.) Vit is another variation of the sun god Seibog, and his partner is Vita or Vida (another variation of Siva). Svantovit is connected with the sun and the crowing rooster, as well as ensuring a bountiful harvest. Since Svantovit was viewed as their supreme deity, his protection was sought going into battle. Svantovit is appealed to in order to avert lightning as well as fevers brought by dog bites and snake bites.

The carving known as the Zbruch Idol is believed to represent Svantovit/Vit's four heads. It is not. If you look closely it is two female heads and two male heads. I speculate that it is the divine couple in

111

Summer (the white time) and Winter (the black time.) Alternative explanations have been that it represents the four seasons, but as I've explained, the ancient Slavs perceived the seasons differently.

Another misinterpretation is that his name means "World-Seer" because *vid* or *vit* means "sight". While the Slavs probably appreciated the play on words, the reason the "Shining Lord of Energy" and the word for "sight" are similar is the same reason in the English language the words "enlighten" and "to see" have commonalities. This play on words is caused by common roots in the Proto-Indo-European language, showing the common concept of energy=light=sight=enlightenment. If Boris Rybakov was correct in translating *vid* in his name to mean sight, that means Sventovit, Jarovit, Rugevit and Porevit would mean Shining Sight, Growing Sight, Red/Roaring Sight and Power Sight. It makes more sense to translate them as The Shining Lord of Energy, The Lord of Growing Energy, The Lord of Raging Energy (war) and The Lord of Power Energy (magic). [All of which they turn out to be.]

From the Victorian era we have recorded a ritual practice left from the worship of Svantovit; a harvest festival that falls around the Autumn Equinox. An authority figure places a rooster onto a wreath made of the newly harvested grains. If the rooster crows, it is considered a sign that next year's harvest will be good and if the rooster remains silent, a bad harvest is predicted. St. Vitus is often depicted with a rooster, a fitting animal for Vid, the "Lord of the Radiant Light." A sculpture of a rooster was put on the top of St. Vitus' Cathedral in Prague, probably built on a former temple to Svantovit. Hence the origin of the prevalent "weathercock" that faces the winds of the four directions.

In a rare description of Moravian Pagan beliefs Svantovit was recorded as "Witislaw." "The god was represented with a gigantick stature [sic] and four faces, beardless, and without hair. The greatest part of the Sclavonians looked upon him as the god of war. He held a large horn in his right hand, and a bow in the left. They kept by him a sword, several arrows, a bridle, a saddle, and a fine white horse, which was carefully fed and curried by the priests. The High-Priest filled the horn with wine every year. When the wine decreased, it was a sign that the next year would prove barren."[22]

Ethnologist Milan Milicevic wrote in the 1880's that on the Summer Solstice (St. Vitus' day) peasant girls would soak the herb *"vidovica"* (Willowherb/ Epilobium) in water and wash their faces with it.

He is a healing god but also a protective war-like god.

Followers: *Vedi*

113

Sacred Day, Time or Holiday: dawn, Spring Equinox, Summer Solstice, Autumn Equinox, Winter Solstice, but especially Summer Solstice, but also the Cross Quarter days May 4-7 to November 5-8.

Sacred Space: hills near water

Sacred Animals: white horse, rooster and hen, bull or ox, black crow, raven

Sacred Plants: grains, Jonny-Jump-Ups (pansies), Blue Cow Wheat, Willow-herb

Sacred Objects: egg, statue of a horse, white horse hair, compass, weather vane, bull's horn, the color red and purple, arm bracelet, drinking horn, solar symbols

Offerings: mead, (better yet, *medovykha* or *miod pitny*) sprouting grains, horns (specifically the horns of any animals you kill), white horse hair

Portable wood god figure circa 9th century Wolin,
Pomerania (now Poland).

Svetovid.

"Svetovid" by Andrej S. Kajsarov from the *Versuch diner Slavischen Mythology* 1804. I would point out that Svantovit's "horn" was more like a drinking horn, rather than a cornucopia. The description by Saxo Grammaticus does have him clean-shaven rather than bearded.

116

A priest of Svantovit depicted at Arkona from a book from 1926 by Carl Schuchhardt. The original carving from about 1150-1200 CE was installed sideways in a wall of a church in Altenkirchen, Germany to signify the triumph of Christianity over Paganism. It is believed to be a depiction of a priest carrying a libation to Svantovit, rather than an image of the four-headed god who was also said to be holding a bow.

Vita (VEET-ah) "Life" (Vida)

She is mainly just remembered as one of the variations of Siva's names and her lore is the same. In the violence of the warrior culture her partner Svantovit was glorified as a warrior and he was worshipped much more than the Goddess of Life.

Sun symbol on the bottom of a vessel from the Transdanubian culture found in Austria. Circa 1500 BCE. Now in the Burgenland Country Museum. Photo by Wolfgang Sauber.

Kupala (koo-PAH-lah) "Lady of Midsummer" -
(Kupajła, Kupal'e, Kupalos, Kupolė, Kostroma)

She is the summertime into winter form of the goddess. Her male partner is Kupalo/Seibog. At the Summer Solstice she is called Marena, because at that point she transforms from the goddess of spring-to-summer (Kupala) and becomes the autumn-thru-winter goddess, Marena.[110] She is also known as Kostroma with her partner, Kostromo.[111] There is some speculation that the name Kupala is a simple confusion of the goddess' name with the name of the holiday. That may be the case, since in Lithuania (one of the last countries to be Christianized) the Midsummer holiday used to be called Kupolės because that was the night that medicinal herbs were picked, an activity called *kupoliavimas*.[112] It is unclear if the name came from the goddess Kupala or the goddess' name came from the holiday. The goddess and god worshipped on Midsummer Night in Lithuania are Lada and Perkunus.[113]

With whatever title you feel comfortable using, this goddess is the representation of the full beauty and bounty of summer. On the sacred night of midsummer, her healing powers are at their greatest and her herbs are the most powerful. So, too, is the love and fertile power between Kupala and her partner, Kupalo. In Latvia, her reign is seen as the time between May until the end of July. She is the goddess of growth, full flowering and peak of summer.

Some of her lore is carried on by St. Agrippina Kupalnitscha (Kupalisko), while her partner's lore falls under St. John the Baptist with the Slavic name of Iwan Kupalnitsch.[37] As St. Agrippina, there is a grotto sacred to her formerly called Contrada Lamia (now called the Cave of St. Agrippina. Lamia in Arabic means "shining" or "radiant".)[114] Lamia is a title associated with both Kupala and Siva. This cave is located in Sicily on one of the highest mountains called Mineo; below it is the river Menas. (We see the sacred combination of most Slavic holy sites: cave, water source and high mountain.)

Agrippina is the patron saint against illness, sea storms and thunderstorms.[115] St. Agrippina is described with blond hair, as the radiant "white" goddess usually is. Although her feast day is unsurprisingly, June 23rd, the Summer Solstice. She is also celebrated during the first weekend of August which would be the time of celebrating the Honey Spas or Harvest celebration.

Sacred Day, Time or Holiday: Summer Solstice (June 21 or 22), August 1st (Medovoy Spas)
Sacred Space: crossroads
Sacred Animals: glow worms or fireflies, ladybugs
Sacred Plants: maidenhair fern, saxifrage, birch, loosestrife

Sacred Objects: wreaths
Offerings: lighting candles, spring water

Fig. 16. — *Adiantum Capillus Veneris.*

Botanical Illustration of a Maidenhair Fern (*Adiantum capillus-veneris*) from a book by Henry Correvon, 1896.

Kupolo (koo-PAH-low) "The Lord of Midsummer" "The Bathed One" (Caloian, German, Kalojan, Kaloyan, Karovit, K'op'ala, Kostromo, Kupajło)

The title of Kupolo is used interchangeably with Jarilo. In The Gods of the Ancient Slavs, Znayenko records Tatishchev's conclusions on this god, "Kupalo is identified as a god of abundance, similar to Ceres in the Hustyn Chronicle, as a god of harvest in the Life, and as a god of the fruits of the earth in the Sinopsis." Tatishchev goes on to describe a ritual of bathing the carving of Kupolo in water on the Summer Solstice.[101] So really, the title of Kupalo just comes from the word *kupat'ska* meaning "to bathe" referring to the ritual of bathing the Lord of Radiant Energy's xoanon in water on his high holy day.

Researcher Louis Potroff cites the similarities between the rain making rituals connected to Jarilo and German to the Russian celebration of Kupalo and the Roumanian "rain-making complex, called *Skaloiian*"[116] or *Caloian*. This celebration is also called Caloian after the god Caloian, Kalojan, Kaloyan, Karovit, all titles of the young spring god. Young girls would make a male doll from clay, rags or dried fruit, usually with a large phallus, and they would process through the fields and around sources of water and finally the figure would be buried or set to float down the river. This ritual was to generate rain. This could also be done on May 12th or the feast of St. Germanus, May 15th.

Kupalo migrated into the culture of the Caucasus mountains as K'op'ala, where he transformed into a semi-deity/ folk hero. He killed lots of ogres and demons, but he also healed physical and mental illnesses. Ritual beer was served at K'op'ala's holy sanctuary and his hops fields were guarded by a giant mythical serpent. In one ballad he transforms into a deer by jumping into a river. Researcher Kevin Tuite also sees a similarity between K'op'ala and St. George, as well.[117] He is certainly seen as a strong, helping supernatural power and is prayed to for protection for travelers and hunters. However, in Georgian beliefs, there is certainly an undercurrent of the patriarchal system going back four or five millennia.

Sacred Day, Time or Holiday: Summer Solstice, Tuesdays
Sacred Space: bright, open wind-swept hills with water nearby
Sacred Animals: white cock, white horse, snake
Sacred Plants: linden (lime) trees, oaks, wild geraniums (cranesbill geranium), cornflowers, white water lilies, mare's-tail, the legendary blooming fern, ivy, asparagus, willows, hazel trees
Sacred Objects: ribbons, flowers, wedding bells, handfasting ribbon or cloth, phallic symbols and sex

toys (in his warrior aspect a sword and shield), staff, keys (especially a golden key)
Offerings: apples, flower wreaths, honey, gold and golden things, grain, beer

Slavic male bronze figure found in Wrocław, Poland. illustration in the Journal of the Association for the Museum of Silesian Antiquities. Vol. VI, 1912. (Creative Commons Attribution-Share Alike license)

124

WINTER

Mora (MOR-ah) or Marzana - (Mar-ZAH-na)

"The Dark Goddess", "The Dream Goddess" (Baba Pethra, Baba Petra, Befana, Behrta, Berchta, Berchte, Berigl, Bertha, Holda, Frau Holda, Frau Perchta, Mara, Marana, Marena, Marmora, Martsyanna, Marza, Marzana, Marzanna, Maslenitsa, Mora, Morana, Morė, Morena, Pehta, Pehta-Baba, Pehtra, Perchta, Salobarda, Smiertka, Wild Bertha, Zlata baba, Zlobna Pehta) -

With her name rooted in the early Slavic *mer-ti*, meaning "the one who kills" she has been described as a "personification of death and winter."[118] People have come up with such varied pictures of her ranging from a "beautiful woman with long black hair, pale white face and wolf-like fangs and claws"[119] to an old woman dressed in white. Yet around 1500 CE, Jan Dlugosz described her as a Slavic Ceres whom farmers honored and offered grain seeds.[120] She has also been compared to the Greek Goddess Hecate, drawing off her connection with magic and the "black" time of the year. Like all the gods and goddesses, Marzana can appear as whatever form she sees fit, but as the elder winter goddess, a depiction of her as an old woman becomes an understandable way to view her.

In Belarus, "Mara" is remembered as a goddess of death. Her name also means "dream" in Belarusian and is the origin of the German word *mare* (as in nightmare.) We see Siva's connection as the Bird Goddess in a South German tradition where if Mara is wound up in the bedsheets and held tightly she will turn into a "white dove" and depart.[121] The Czech and some other Slavic peoples use Mora's name for "moth";[122] one of the common forms she can take. This goes back to the belief that the soul can leave the body in sleep or when witches astral travel.

In Germany we see the *Mahri* or *Mohr*, as "riders of the storm." Their names connect them to the Slavic goddess, Mora. An unnamed Victorian scholar talks about Indra's attendants who were "spirits of the wind, whose hosts are partly composed of the souls of the dead. These riders of the storm were named *Maruts*. He goes on to say they were degraded to witches and explained their connection with the sieve. "The rain-drops descending from the clouds suggested water poured through a sieve, and hence the sieve early became a symbol of the clouds; and as the *Muruts*, the wind-spirits, rode upon their clouds… so the sieve was the chosen vehicle of the mares and witches wherein to be wafted over sea and land." He also connects the Indian wind spirits to the Wild Hunt,[123] which Mora's German counterpart, Petra, is connected to as well. The magical use of the sieve for rain-making would have also come from Mora.

126

It is said that if you are not afraid of her, she will appear as a beautiful young woman clad in white. If you hold a cyclical worldview, death is not the end, but simply a resting time spent with spirits and gods until one is reborn anew. This can be frightening to some and because Marzana embodies these powers she can be seen with fear and loathing. To those who are not afraid, death can be a beautiful goddess who welcomes you into her arms to rest. In Latvia, she is remembered as the "mother of all", the Creatrix. While it may seem counterintuitive, since Marzana is mainly remembered as a "Death Goddess" she is the portal between the spirit world and the world of the living. She is the Goddess of Death but she is also the Goddess of Rebirth. In the cycle of the natural world, Marzana metamorphoses into Devana, her youthful spring form. This is celebrated in the spring holiday of Maslenitsa, where an effigy of the winter goddess is ritually burnt.

In Latvia, her symbol is a geometric backward "S" symbolising *zalktis*, the adder. In the lore there, "Mara" can transform into the healing snake, often a white snake, so this symbol is embroidered on women's clothes to hold Mara's protection. While in Bulgaria, the goddess is associated with the cat. In the seasonal transition of the mummer's parade, a man dressed as "Grandmother" ("Mara") will enact giving birth and bring forth a live kitten. Her lore is carried on by St. Gertrude, the patron saint of cats, with her feast day around the Spring Equinox. The saint is depicted spinning and surrounded by mice. [124] Mice, shrews, and moles were sacred to the goddess of the Underworld since they lived under the earth.

Just as there are "white women" and shining vila who are like minor versions of the White Goddess, there are *mora, zmoras, morava, moroi* who are lesser spirits or magic workers like Mora.[122] From her name of Pehtra Baba, her followers are called *pehtra*, while a variation of that would be the Germanic *perchtas*.

Followers: *pehtra, mora, zmoras, morava, moroi, sorginak* Basque: *Sorginak, Maindi, Maide, Mairi*
Sacred Day, Time or Holiday: Wednesdays and between the Winter Solstice and Spring Equinox
Sacred Space: crossroads, caves
Sacred Animals: cat, dog, fish, snakes, lizard, toad, goose, crow, ravens, owl, ladybug, weasel, hedgehog, mice, shrews, red horse, red ram, black billy goat
Sacred Plants: fungi, mushrooms, yew tree, celery
Sacred Objects: sieve, sickle, spindle, spindle whorls, distaff, black wool, goddess figures carved on white stone or bone, deer teeth, triangular bone pendants, red ochre
Offerings: blackberries, flax, hemp or other fiber, milk, unleavened bread or porridge, poppy seeds

128

Symbol: An "x" formed from four "x's" or a cross formed from four crosses; a backward "S".

Burning Mazlentsa by A.M. Vasnetsov 1920 in the Moscow Regional Museum.

Death Goddess lifting her skirts so all can return to her womb. This Goddess figure 3800-3600 BCE was found in the Ghelăieşti Sanctuary. Now in the Piatra Neamt Museum. Photo by Cristian Chirita.

Hors - (chors) "The Dark God" - (Beržulis, Chors, Corsa, Hars, Harsh, Hawrs, Hers, Herson, Hors, Hors Dazbog, Horse, Horsun, Horz, Hrs, Hurs, Karachun, Kherson, Khors, Khors Dazbog, Khoros, Khros, Khursun, Kopc, Korcha, Korochun, Kors, Korsa, Korscha, Kors Dazbog, Korssa, Korsun, Krachun, Kračún, Kūčios, Kuču, Marowit, Marzaniok, Xopc, Xors, Xorutani, Xŭrs Daž'bog, Xŭrsŭ)

Hors or Khors is the winter name of Dazbog and can also be known by the composite name of Hors-Dazbog. Hors aka Korochun is "resurrected" and becomes Koleda on the Winter Solstice.[125] To the Scythians he was known as Khursun.[126] The Wends have a god named Marowit meaning **"Lord of Nightmares"**[127] which I think obviously connects to Hors. Researcher Vesna Kakaševski writes that the Czech word for fire is *horecka*, and a rooster can be called an *oroz*, both words connect Hors to the Radiant Lord of Light.[128] Stamatovic goes on to say that there is also *xorovod*, a type of sacred dance. Additionally, *Horos, khoros* and *choros* all mean "dance" in the Greek language. Goran Pavlovik points out what makes this really interesting is that it connects to the harvest of grain with the circular *chorostasi*, the Greek threshing floor where they would dance.[129]

In the Edwardian era, "Chors" was recognized as a "god of the harvest".[18] The island of Khortytsya on the Dnieper river in Ukraine, got its name from the sacred dogs or *Hort* which protected the Pagan temple of Hors on this island.[130] An ancient description from the *De Administrando Imperio* states that the Rus when they got to this island, "they perform their sacrifices because a gigantic oak-tree stands there: and they sacrifice live cocks. Arrows, too, they peg in round about, and others bread and meat, or something of whatever each may have, as is their custom. They also throw lots regarding the cocks, whether to slaughter them, or to eat them as well, or to leave them alive."[131] According to tales he owns a fire-breathing winged horse, lives on a mountain surrounded by ice and snow and has ravens and other birds of "ill omen".

Followers: *Čert* or the fey *chors* or *chort*
Sacred Day, Time or Holiday: January 14th, Solstices and Equinoxes
Sacred Space: hills and mountains
Sacred Animals: white horse, wolf, boar, dog, dragon, fire-breathing winged horse, ravens, cock
Sacred Plants: grains, celery, holly, oak
Sacred Objects: anvil, blacksmithing tools, sun symbols, metal ore, boar tusk, stone with a hollow
Offerings: candle, bread, coal, gold, silver, gemstones, water from a blacksmith's forge, rain water, black cock
Sacred Objects: sieve, sickle, spindle, spindle whorls, distaff, black wool, goddess figures carved on white stone or bone, deer teeth, triangular bone pendants, red ochre

Offerings: blackberries, flax, hemp or other fiber, milk, unleavened bread or porridge, poppy seeds

"Stone Scythian" a Kurgan stelae on Khortytsia Island. Photo by Irina Shatova. (Creative Commons Attribution-Share Alike license)

133

"Stone Scythian" a Kurgan stelae on Khortytsia Island. Photo by Irina Shatova. (Creative Commons Attribution-Share Alike license)

Korent - (KHOR-ent) "The Sky Father",
"Master of Animals," "Wolf Shepherd" -
(Casuantanus, Caruantanus, Chors, Chorutani, Chorz, Çura, Czur, Hors, Kalojan, Kaloyan, Karant, Karatan, Karevit, Karewit, Karotan, Karovit, Keremet, Kerons, Khursu, Korant, Kore, Koreta, Korotan, Kurent, Xorutani, Xors)

At some point the lore of Korent and Hors separated and their qualities are enough different that I am listing them separately, yet if you look at the name variations you can see there are essentially the same. Yet, Korent is remembered as a merrier figure than Hors.

Historian Jožko Šavli explains that "Korant" is known as "The Sky Father," "Master of Animals," or "Wolf Shepherd." Šavli also explains that his origins are from misty prehistory. He was "The Great Spirit" in the time of the hunter/gatherers. He was pictured with reindeer and bison horns and he is still accompanied in spring and winter rituals with mummers in animal masks showing his role as "Master of the Animals." He is also the main god, "father of his people," essentially the same as Dazbog.[132] He is the Horned God, just as Veles is depicted.

Linguist Davorin Trstenjak writes, "Slovene: Kres, Kresnik, is also called Çura, and his name means the same as Kerons." He goes on to explain that Kerons can also be found in the variations of the name Korant. Trstenjak mentions a Polabian [German/Polish] monument to Karovit, who is definitively connected to the God of the Radiant Light because of his symbolism of a bull's head and cock.[25] In fact, Monika Kropej points out *kura* means chicken in Slovene.[73] Karvit was known to the Polabians as Gerovit, another name for the Spring god Jarilo, Korent's youthful form.

Monika Kropej cites Janez Bilc's recorded folk tale of the Slovenian "Kurent" and points out that the grapevine and the buckwheat grain is sacred to him. He is also the god of wine and revelry. In folktales Kurent plays a flute so enticingly that people can't help but keep dancing to it and even Death is made to dance.[132]

In Serbia the Radiant God of Fertility is reduced to the character of The Plowman in the Carnival who is called Korant, Korent, or Kurent.[25] Korent and his goddess partner are served by the horned and hairy *kurenti*, who show up in the Carnival parades.

According to the Slovene National Benefit Society the *kurenti* have horns, sticks for whiskers, long red tongues and are decorated with streamers and feathers. Young girls present their handkerchiefs to the *kurenti* and that is added to their belts along with their clanking bells. In an interesting tradition, "the people of the town smash clay pots at the feet of the *kurents* for good luck and good health."[133]

The ancient *koribanti* were dressed in the masks of a rooster.[19] The symbol of the rooster connecting to his aspect of the "Sun God," just as Vit's (Svantovit) symbol is the rooster. This spring tradition got moved to the Winter Solstice, when the "New Year" dates were changed. Hence you will still see the miming of the rooster, hen and chicks incorporated into Serbian Christmas traditions.

Korent in winter is known as the "Master of Animals" and the "Wolf Shepherd," who starts his rule at the end of October/beginning of November. As such, Jožko Šavli connects him to St. Martin who is greatly revered in the same Slovenian territory that Korent was.[132]

Linguist Davorin Trstenjak writes that the medieval monk Nestor recorded the name of Korent as "Xorutani and Chorutani."[25] We have seen the shortened form recorded as Xors, Chors, and Hors. As "Chors" he is regarded as "god of the harvest."[18] Thus I would identify the goddess companion of Korent/Chors as the winter goddess Mora and it is for her that the traditional goose is sacrificed on St. Martin's Day. We also see a goose "sacrificed" and traditionally eaten on Michaelmas, St. Michael's Day. This festival is celebrated on various dates (September 29th, October 4th, and

October 11th)[134] depending on the climate and probably spread with the Celts into Europe.

There are also "devils" or "goblins" known as *chors* or *chort*. These are horned creatures that get into mischief. They are also called *bes* or *bjes* and their leader is called Bjesomar or Rampogusto, which translates to "Cherish-goblin" the one who cares for the "goblins".[26]

We also see the remnants of the merry god Korent and his horned *kurenti* preserved in the lore of St. Nicholas who travels around Slovenia on December 6th with his *parklji*, mischievous elves and *hudici*, [135] horned creatures who of course are now known as "devils." On the Eve of December 6th, children set out plates, shoes or stockings to receive the gifts of the saint. While we have no written records of the time before the Christians came, it is not a stretch to think that this tradition probably started with the god Kurent bestowing dried fruits and nuts (which were the traditional "gifts.") Much like the German Krampus, the horned *hudici* stuff naughty children into a basket or give them a stick.

While it used to be that the horned god Korent had reindeer antlers or bison horns, now our merry grandfather-figure of Santa is pulled by reindeer instead. Just like the *kurenti*, Santa "was dressed all in fur from his head to his toes" but the Victorian image reduced it down to just a bit of fur trim. The

music and noisy bells that chased away winter, now brighten the Winter Solstice & Christmas.
Practitioner Anna Urosevic Applegate writes that during the winter season wolf magic was especially strong, "It was assumed that spirit wolves were everywhere, and your behavior toward them would affect how you'd be treated by real wolves, as well as how the spirits would treat you." If they were to share this information with Kurent the "Wolf Shepherd," it brings a whole new perspective to "he knows if you've been bad or good, so be good for goodness sake!"[1]

Followers: *kurenti, koribanti, chort, chors, bes, Corybants, Korybantes, Kurbantes.*
Sacred Day, Time or Holiday: Tuesdays, Autumn Equinox, November 11th (although more accurately Nov. 7th or October 31st) December 6th, & the Winter Solstice, Spring Equinox
Sacred Space: hill
Sacred Animals: rooster, goat, bull, bear, wolf, boar, ox
Sacred Plants: apples, yellow "Corn Marigold," grapevine, buckwheat, blackberries
Sacred Objects: spoked "sun wheels", flute, fiddle
Offerings: golden apples, wine, cooked buckwheat, grapes, wheat sheaves

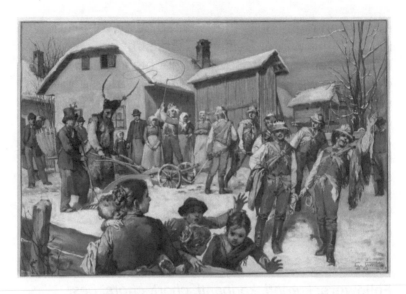

"Der Zug der Pflüger" (The Plow Train) with horned
Korent by Jurij Šubic, 1890.

"Dedek Mraz" (Grandfather Cold) - illustration by
Maksim Gaspari in the Slovenian Ethnographic
Museum, Ljubljana, Slovenia.
photo by author

Korencia - (KHOR-ent-chah)"Mother of the Animals" - (Bendis, Cibela, Cybebe, Cybele, Kibela, Kibelia, Katys, Kubaba, Kubeleya, Kurecija, Kybele, Kybele, Potnia, Rhea, Sybil)

Korent is not usually mentioned with a female counterpart, yet when we look where this hole in our knowledge is we would be looking for the female form of Korent... something like Kurentia. I didn't find that spelling but I found a mention of "Kurecija". Researcher Slavko Ciglenečki quotes the 13th century author, Thomas Archidiakonus, "Croatia used to be named *Kurencija*, and the nations which are now called Croatians used to be called *Kuretes* or *Koribantes*."[136] I'll point out that Austria, Germania, Britannia, and Éire/Ériu, are all named after goddesses, so it would make sense that "Croatia" was the same. Another interesting clue that this goddess existed is the word *kurecia* which means chicken in Slovak. Ciglenečki points out the priests of Cybele's cult were called *galli* (roosters) and in Bulgaria the Kurent is surrounded by children dressed as *piceki* (cockerels). Both *galli* and *piceki* wear a type of pointed hat or "Phrygian cap".[136]

Monika Kropej writes, "Let us also consider a Slovene folk Carnival custom in which the *kurenti*, accompanied by a procession of the *piceki* (chicks) jump up and down and "plough" around houses to make their owner's turnips grow thick and plump. The latest archaeological discoveries revealed the

142

connection between the *kurenti* and the ancient cult of Cybele, according to which the mythical companions of Cybele were called the *kurenti* and the *koribanti* (Ciglenecki 1999.)"[73]

In Slovenia, originally only young, unmarried males could play the *kurenti* but now everyone gets in on the fun. This is celebrated in the spring "Carnival" season before Lent, but was probably originally on either the Spring Solstice or May 6th (May Day). While parading around the *kurenti* have to jump high to bring about tall fertile crops.

Cybele is also understood to be the same goddess as Rhea. Rhea is described at Theoi.com:
In all European countries Rhea was conceived to be accompanied by the *Curetes...* and in Phrygia by the *Corybantes, Atys,* and *Agdistis*. The *Corybantes* were her enthusiastic priests, who with drums, cymbals, horns, and in full armour, performed their orgiastic dances in the forests and on the mountains of Phrygia. The lion was sacred to the mother of the gods, because she was the divinity of the earth, and because the lion is the strongest and most important of all animals on earth..." (comp. Ov. Met. x. 682)."[137] Rhea was usually shown seated on a throne with lions on both sides of her.

Morana transforms to Vesna in the spring. Since Vesna is the partner of Kresnik, and Korent is Kresnik's winter form, that means Kurecija is the same goddess as Morana. Morana is described as living in a "mirror palace" which seems to me that this refers to her winter realm of ice and snow.

Her mortal followers would have reached an ecstatic state and then prophesied or healed.

Followers: *kurenti, koribanti, chort, chors, bes, Corybantes, Corybants, Korybantes, Kurbantes.*
Sacred Day, Time or Holiday: Tuesdays, Autumn Equinox, November 11th (although more accurately Nov. 7th or October 31st) December 6th, & the Winter Solstice, Spring Equinox
Sacred Space: hill
Sacred Animals: hen, sow, lions, pelicans, cranes, storks
Sacred Plants: apples, yellow "Corn Marigold," grapevine, buckwheat, blackberries
Sacred Objects: throne, magnetic iron, iron rings, porphryry
Offerings: golden apples, wine, cooked buckwheat, grapes

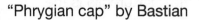

"Phrygian cap" by Bastian

144

Cybele, Ceres and Flora on a chariot surrounded by many forms of natural abundance, *corybantes* and cherubs, symbolizing the element earth. Engraving by A. Tempesta, 1592.

Mat Zemla - (maht-ZEM-lah)"Damp

Mother Earth" - (Baubo, Curche, Hertha, Gabjauga, Gorche, Gurche, Kurch, Kurcha, Kurka, Kurek, Kussus, Majka Vlazna Zemlja, Mata Syra Zemlja, Mata Syra Zjemlja, Mati Syra Zemia, Matka Syra Zjemlja, Matka Ziema, Matka Ziemia, Matka Ziema, Matka Zeme, Matkę Ziemię, Matki Ziemi, Mati Syra Zemlia, Mati Syra Zemlya, Mati Zemlya, Matushka Zemlia, Mother Earth Syra, Nëna Tokë, Semele, Semmesmaat, Semyna, Žemelė, Zeme Mate, Žemė Pati, Zemepati, Zemes maate, Žemina, Zemynele, Zemyna, Žytniamatka)

The version of her name "Mati Syra Zemlya" literally means "Damp Mother Earth."[138] Zemyna means "earth" so she is also called Semyna or Zeme Mate, "Mother Earth," or she could be perceived as **"Baba,"** the "old woman." Boris Čok writes that "In the Slovene Kras region and the Italian Liguria, if a child fell on the floor, people would say that it kissed the baba/old woman…"[78] Even in the early Middle Ages, Mat Zemla was still recognized as a powerful goddess. She is bountiful and giving, as well as all-receiving. In Lithuanian Pagan prayers she is poetically referred to as Ziedkele, **"She Who Raises Flowers."**[139]

Mother Earth was sacred and oaths were made touching the ground, putting earth on your head or swallowing a lump of earth. Even in the Middle Ages, if you couldn't get to confession it was considered acceptable to confess your sins into a hole in the earth and then fill in the hole. In the same manner, you could bury your illness by digging a hole and giving it to the Earth Mother to transform.

It is speculated that the word *zmei* meaning serpent comes from *zemlia*, meaning "earth".[140] We see Neolithic figurines of snake goddesses, and snakes with female attributes. In some Lithuanian sources you will see the snake connected with "Zemininkas, god of agriculture."[141] At first I thought this was a male-centric interpretation written by the medieval priest Maciej Stryjkowski, but I now think that Zemininkas is Mat Zemla's god partner. This seems to be confirmed with the Encyclopaedia of Religion and Ethics writing, "Zemynele was held to be the sister of Zemepattys (Praetorius, p. 31) They received worship in common."[142] (Since the divine couple are both siblings and lovers.) Their festival was held at the end of October and at the Winter Solstice.

With dirt floors and warm cook stoves, house snakes were common. The snake was honored in the home and often fed omelets or milk. Among the Letts, they were called *peena maates*, "mothers of milk."[142] While many chroniclers interpreted this as "snake worship," that would be like saying Christians do "bread worship" in the form of the host. The snake was an emissary or even a manifestation of the goddess in the home and was treated as an honored guest. In Lithuanian paganism the grass snake is revered as an envoy of the gods.

Offerings of hemp oil or beer is made at each of the four directions or at each corner of a field to honor the Earth Mother. Sows were also sacrificed to Žemina.[143] At weddings and at the harvest, the celebrant would spill some beer on the ground as a libation to Žemina, say a prayer to her and then drink the rest. A rooster or hen would be sacrificed to the goddess and then cooked. Each member of the family would get a loaf of bread, give a prayer or blessing over the loaf and eat it along with the meat. The bones and any bread scraps would be ritually buried in the earth. As Curche (Gorcho, Gurcho, Kurko) she was the benefactor of all food and drink and so to her was sacrificed the first grains, bread, flour, honey, beans, milk, mead and beer.[144]

As the earth goddess, she is also a death goddess, who welcomes the dead back into her. She is the goddess of the whole cycle of birth, life, death, and the fallow resting time before being reborn. She is also the goddess of the harvest. Farmers kiss the earth good morning and again at night.

In Germany, Belarus & Russia, Žemina's lore is carried on in the lore of St. Sophia. This helps us identify one of the goddess' traits, that of holy wisdom. Adding weight to her as a goddess of the watery Underworld is a little plant called herb-Sophia.

148

In Germany the plant is named after St. Sophia (aka "Cold Sophia") who is prayed to to prevent late frosts. In Slovenia, the saint is called *mokra Zofija* meaning "Wet Sophia".[145] This same plant is known in Lithuania and is named after Poklius, the god of the underworld. St. Sophia's holy day is May 15 which is considered to be the last day of winter in some European areas.

Followers:
Sacred Day, Time or Holiday: May 6th (May Day), August 15th (or the harvest festival of Dożynki), end of October, Winter Solstice
Sacred Space: openings in the earth, caves (especially vulva shaped caves), large flat stones on hills and mountains
Sacred Animals: snake, cows, black pig (sows), black birds: black hens, ravens, crows, etc.
Sacred Plants: motherwort, hemp, herb-Sophia
Sacred Objects: earth, vulva-shaped stones, red ochre, the color black
Offerings: hemp oil, red ochre, libations poured on the earth (wine, beer, ale, milk, water), bread buried in the earth, black feathers, sheaf of grain

"Kamienna baba" (Baba Stone) in Neple, Poland by Miedzionikiel, 2020 (Creative Commons Attribution-Share Alike license)

Zemepatis - (zeh-meh-PAT-ees)"Father

Earth" - (Curcho, Hertho, Gabjaugo, Gorcho, Gurcho, Kurch, Kurcho, Kurko, Kurchus, Kurek, Kussus, Poklius, Raugo Zameluks, Zemeluksztis, Žemėpatis, Raugupatis, Rugutis, Zemélō, Zemepatis, Zemepattys, Zemininkas, Zempattys, Zemypatie, Ziemiennikas)

Author Michael Strmiska states both that "Zemepatis is the male counterpart to Zemepati," and later he states that Zemyna is the earth goddess and "Zemepatis, the brother of Zemyna and protector of the household."[146] I have seen over and over that the divine couple is both siblings and lovers. This deity is probably the most combined in its genders, probably because of being the earth itself.

Like his female counterpart, he is closely connected to snakes. In the Encyclopaedia of Religion and Ethics it states, "Zemynele was held to be the sister of Zemepattys (Praetorius, p. 31) They received worship in common." Their festival was held at the end of October and at the Winter Solstice.[147] James Hastings sums up the account recorded by 16th century priest Jan Lasicki, "On the shortest day a festival was held in honour of Zempattys, 'the god of farms and farmhouses' in the course of which 'each takes his bread, presses it to the ground and speaks: "O Zemypatie, thou givest us such good bread, we thank thee for it. Help us to cultivate our

151

fields with thy blessing, and through the co-operation [sic] of Zemynele to receive more of thy good gifts."

As "Zemininkas" he is perceived as the "god of agriculture". Gloria Kivytaite O'Brien writes, "Raugo Žemėpatis, Rugutis or Raugupatis was the deity of sourdough, leaven and fermentation. He governed the baking of bread and the brewing of beer, as well as wine and other similar products. People would sacrifice the first swallow of fresh beer, and the first loaf of bread."[148]

His ancient images have been described as "the Thinker" or the "Sorrowful God" as he contemplates the cycle of life and death.

Followers:
Sacred Day, Time or Holiday: May 6th (May Day), August 15th (or the harvest festival of Dożynki), end of October/beginning of November, Winter Solstice
Sacred Space: openings in the earth, caves (especially vulva shaped caves)
Sacred Animals: snake, bulls, black boar, black birds: black rooster, ravens, crows, etc.
Sacred Plants: hemp, herb-Sophia
Sacred Objects: earth, red ochre, the color black
Offerings: hemp oil, red ochre, libations poured on the earth (wine, beer, milk, water), bread buried in the earth, black feathers, sheaf of grain, honey cakes

"The Thinker" - Hamangia culture from Romania;
circa 5000 BC. Photo by 三猎 2016 (Creative
Commons Attribution-Share Alike license)

Ʋᴇlᴇꙅ (Vel-ES) "The Ruler", "Lord of the Dead"
"Lord of the Fairies" "The Lord of the Underworld"
"Master of Animals", "Wolf Shepherd"- (Bábilon,
Babylon, Balinis, Báron Bálon, Barowit, Bedanec,
Bekelnis, Benec, Berstuk, Bés, Bevardis, Birutes, Bor,
Borovik, Boruta, Borewit, Busó, Busók, Črt, Esus,
Gabikis, Goniglis Dziewos, Hades, Hesuls, Hesus,
Kalvelis, Kaukarus, Kaukas, Krakonoš, Kuznets,
Lintvern, Moran, Patelo, Patols, Pecols, Peorevid,
Perovit, Picollos, Picullus, Pikol, Pikulas Velnias,
Pluto, Pocols, Poklus, Pokoie, Porevid, Pore-Vit,
Porevithus, Potollo, Potoglav, Pripegalis, Ragius,
Roszkas, Stepans, Stribor, Swiatibor, Teliavelis,
Teljaevi, Teljavel, Tjarnaglofi, Tolovaj, Tolovaj iz
Velenja, Trdoglav, Vanapagan, Vedius, Veive, Veiovis,
Vejovis, Velas, Vēlenas, Velez, Velikan, Velinas,
Vēlinas, Velinus, Velnias, Velns, Vels, *Velunas, Vetisl,
Vjeles, Viales, Vilez, Vilnius, Voden, Volos, Vouvel
(Vouvel the Giant), Vulcan, Wawel, Weles, Wels,
Wieles, Zmaj, Zorngott, Zuttibur)

It can be startling how many different titles Veles has.
(And I've only listed about half of the ones that I've
gathered.) Along with spelling variations and
language variations you also have titles proliferating
because of the "power of the word". If you think
about it… no one wanted to call upon "Death" and
invoke him so consequently many euphemisms were
used.

In Lithuania, he is known as Teliavelis or Kalvelis and *kalvelis* means "smith: or son of the smith."[149] So we know Veles is a blacksmith (just like Svarog and Hors-Dazbog). I believe Veles/Volos became "Wayland the Smith" (Wolund) in Northern European lore. Ralston gives us another of his names when he mentions a song that is done at the Winter Solstice which calls upon the divine blacksmith, Kuznets" - "the Slavonic Vulcan, who became transformed in Christian times into the double saint Kuz'ma-Dem'yan [Cosmas and Demian]."[6] Kuznets is associated with snakes, guarded by two wolves and he takes men to the underworld.[150] Demian may be Veles' springtime form. It's important to know that these saints were healing saints, so Veles is a healer. It is stressed that these healing saints never took any money for their services, so followers of Veles who heal shouldn't ask for money (although gifts are traditionally offered).

Another possible origin of Veles' name comes from clues from Valaam Island in Russia originally occupied by the Finno-Ugric peoples. There was worship there of Veles and Perun and the islands were described as "a giant pagan altar." They state that Veles may have come from Beles, a variation of Baal.[151] Whereas, his name variation of Pecols, corresponds with the god Pluto. This variation also gives us Puck and the Celtic *pooka*. A variation of Pecols is the Prussian Patols/Patulas which comes from *pa meaning "under" and *tula meaning "earth."[149]

These theories mainly focus on linguistics without actually comprehending the god and all his lore. After looking at all these theories, I think it is simply that Veles has the same root as "spirit" because Veles is the Lord of the Spirits (the Dead). The Victorian author, A. von Ulrich writes, "*Vele* is the Lettish name for the soul; and the grass, the turf as covering the tombs of the dead is called *Velna*. In both words 'V' has been changed into 'S,' and *Sielen* in Russian is the name for grass, and *Seele* in German is soul." (And remember that the Celtic fairies are called the Seelie Court and Veles is Lord of the Fey.) Von Ulrich goes on to say that the Devil is called Wels and "thus the benevolent protector of the departed has been turned into an evil spirit."[28] I agree with Ivanov and Toporov who believe the name of Veles originates with the Indo-European word *vel-*, which means "the dead" or spirit. (From which stems the name of *Valhalla*, the Norse abode of the valorous dead.) However, I disagree with them that Veles is connected to Vedic "demons" but rather, as Ivankovic proposes, he is like the wise god Veruna of India.

Veles is closely connected to marshes, moors and even puddles,[152] but he can also be found traveling in a gust of wind. He loves the woodland and the energy of large rocks. He is also to be found at crossroads at midnight. Wells are sacred to him and are seen as entry points to the Underworld. He can be invoked by whistling at a crossroads or whistling in the home.

Veles is the Lord of the Fey: the fairy *Veela (Vile),* the woodland *Barstukai*, the forest *Leshi* and the dwarf-like *Kaukai*. Like the *Leshi*, the hairy woodland spirits, Veles can change his size. He can be seen as a young child, a dwarf, a youth, a man, an old woman or a giant in folktales. In the Karkonosze Mountains, he takes the form of a man with a bull's head.[147] He carries a staff and connects to people in their dreams in a shamanic manner. Veles is mentioned in the *Slovo* as the "grandfather" of popular poets and singers and Anichkov points out that "the author seems to consider him a peaceful god and a patron of the arts."[153] In eastern Lithuania, he is called *Goniglis Dziewos* meaning the **"God of Herds"**. He was prayed to to guard the herds from wolves and other predators.[77]

Veles carries a set of bagpipes,[5] showing his connection to the bardic roles of musicians, poets, and singers. In the Song of Igor's Band he is said to be the grandfather of *boiany* or bards,"[77] patron of musicians, poets and those with the gift of prophecy. Combining his connection with bards, and also with the woods, he would be the god of the Slavic druidic priests and priestesses. They had the power to sing the future into being and shape the world through words, just as Veles does. Veles is the patron of

157

magic workers and visionaries who tap into the powers of the unconscious realm; shamanic journeying, shape changing, the collective unconscious, and visioning. Indeed, the word *volkhv'* or *volhov*, in some Slavic languages means "magician" or "sorcerer" and is believed to derive from his name. With his title of Ragius, we can see that he is a teacher of magic and prophecy, *regēti* meaning "to see". In the Baltic lands Velinas is one-eyed.[152] There are many clues that lead me to believe the worship of Veles (Weles) evolved into that of Woden. In Veles' Lithuanian name variation of Velinas, he is seen as the creator of the raven, crow, reptiles, and wolves. He's described as having a limp. In Latvia "Velns" is depicted in folktales as having one human leg and one leg that of a horse or cow.[154] This shows how he evolved into the Germanic Krampus who also has one human leg and one leg with a cloven hoof.

In Lithuania Veles is connected to horses, oxen, cows and goats, but also the wild animals of the forest especially the wolf, rabbit, and bear into which he transforms. Although he can also take the form of a black cat, black or white rooster. Additionally he has been described as taking the form of black dog, black pig, a black bug, black bird, or a huge fish (pike or perch). He can even take the form of a whirlwind. Whirlpools and wells can be the entrance to his Underworld kingdom, so gifts to him are offered there.

Veles' most common incarnation is that of a dragon. Thus in Christianity it became an evil symbol. Many ancient magic workers (usually male) were respected as "Dragon men" having the blood of a shape-shifting dragon in their lineage giving them magic powers. So in Christian lore a dragon became "a magical serpent, a fiend who can impersonate a handsome man or even a husband or lover, and thereby entrap a woman."[155] These "Dragon men" (and women) are shamans who work with Veles. Just as we call the insects that frequent ponds a dragonfly, in Lithuania they refer to them as "Velinas's horses".[152]

In Lithuania, Velinas can appear as a flying, fiery or crowned snake. His symbol of the snake connects to his shamanic role. Gimbutas writes, "A person who received his crown would become clairvoyant and omniscient, would see hidden treasures, and would understand animal language." I believe this is what is meant in tales when they talk about "eating the white snake," awakening what in India would be called the *kundalini* energy. A way to describe the shamanic initiation that results in awakening magical powers.

Followers: véščii, *volx, vol'ga, volkhv'* or *balabántar, bédanec, bédou'nk, benandant, krewe, Krive, krivevto, kriwait, krywody, kunigas, kodlaci,* (high priest *Krewes-Kreweito, Krewe-Krewejto* or *Grive Grivaito* meaning "Judge of Judges") *ujédemec,* *vaidilos (pl), vaidutis, védamec, védancvédavec, vedavci (pl), védavk, vedomci, vedomec, vedúnec, véjdamec, vermánte, véšča, vidence, vidovina, vlah, volhov, vukodlak, wołchw or wołchwa (f), waydlot, waidolotten, Waidolotten (pl f) or boiany (bards),* his fey servants are *vēlés (the vile), veli, velniai or potorochy.*

If you know him as Kaukas then you would interact with his dwarfish servants *kaukai* and as a priest/ess be called a *kaukucones.* If you call him Berstuk, his woodland spirits are *barstukas* or *barstukai* and if you call him Leshy, you would interact with his spiritual servants the woodland *leshi.*

Sacred Day, Time or Holiday: Wednesdays, Saturdays (although Saturday might be his feminine partner's day) & February 2nd (or Feb. 12th), Veija Noc (Great Night) especially the Winter Solstice and the Days of the Dead around November 2nd-5th.

Sacred Space: forests, wooded river banks, barn, pastures, places of commerce such as a market, low places, caves, underground springs, islands, under an elderberry bush, sometimes the tops of hills and mountains

Sacred Animals: ram, black sheep, bear, wolf, lynx, bull, dog, snake, dragon, reptiles, aurochs, cattle, horse, black birds (raven, crow, grebe), wren, dragonfly, moth

Sacred Plants: walnut tree, rowan tree, willow, cedar, holly, ivy, mistletoe, a wheat sheaf, wheat, corn or other grains, basil, woodland herbs, wormwood, giant fennel (Ferula), elderberry, herb-Sophia, mosses (especially club moss), burdock, root plants (such as beets, turnips, etc.)

Sacred Objects: a forked staff or a shepherd's staff, horns (ram, goat, or bull), black key, (gate of the Underworld,) flute (especially a *sopilka*), bagpipes, *gusli*, boat, ammonite fossil, blacksmithing tools, anvil, three skulls (human, ox and horse)

Offerings: bread (bread and salt), eggs, omelets, walnuts, mead or other sweet, heavy wine or fruit cordials, beer, cowbell, animal musks, black fur, black wool, carvings of skulls, music, coins of precious metals, gems or raw ore, jet, obsidian, onyx, cedar incense, blacksmithed iron, poetry

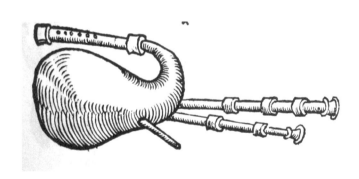

"Bagpipe" Martin Agricola; *Musica Instrumentalis Deudsch*, 1529.

"Buso" at Hungarian Carnival. Photo by Arkinessa 2020 (Creative Commons Attribution-Share Alike license)

Veliona (vel-LON-yah) "Goddess of Souls" or "Goddess of the Dead" (Babilonia, Giltine, Helene, Kapinių žmogus, Kaulinyčia, Kolera, Laume, Nia, Nija, Nya, Nyamos, Nyi, Nyja, Nyji, Nyjz, Maras, Maro mergos, Pavietre, Plutona, Quia, Ragaine, Ragana, Tija, Veliuona, Vellone, Vielona, Velu maate, Welenā, Welli-Deewa, Wellon, Wellona, Wellone, Žie žara, Žie žula, Žie žula-Ragana, Žverūna)

In Lithuania she is known as the **"Goddess of the Forefathers' Shadows"**[156] essentially the Goddess of the Ancestors' Spirits. The ancient Prussians called her Giltine as "the superior over the dead."[36] There she is identified as the "sister" of Laima (Siva/Diva) and in a role like the Grim Reaper. The Latvians called her Welli-Deewa. Just like the Poles perceived Devanna and Marzanna as the white goddess and the black goddess trading places and ruling different times of the year it would seem that the Latvians recognized this duality in Welli-Deewa putting together the names of the Dark Goddess, Veliona and the White Goddess, Diva. Thus Veliona is essentially the Queen of the Spirits and the Underworld, same as Marzanna/Morena.

She would also be the Queen of the Fairies (*Vile*), as well as Queen of the Snakes. Her name of Ragana means "to see" or "to divine" plus *ragas* means "horn" as in the "moon's horn" or the crescent moon.

163

[58] Her name of Nyji means to "dry, wither, disappear, die".[157]

While the title of Veliona isn't technically Slavic since her name is only known in the Latvian, Lithuanian and Baltic regions, she is a much better match for Veles (known in the Balkans as Velnias.) These Baltic beliefs mirror the Slavs with Perkunas as the Lord of Thunder and Laima, as the Goddess Siva. Veliona's name means "Goddess of Souls."[66] She is the Dark Mother welcoming spirits to rest in the watery Underworld, or sending them forth to be reborn. She is also seen as the goddess of eternity and future life. When the Latvian culture was known as Lettish, they worshipped Zemes maate, which literally means "earth mother." It is also noted in that culture that her role as "ruler of the dead" was merged with "Velu maate."[139] Although Velu maate means "mother of the dead" you can see the similarity to Veles, since *velu* means "dead."

She is Queen of the Fairies (the *Vila*) just as Veles is the King of the Fairies. Just as Celtic fairies are sometimes thought to be the souls of the dead, the Slavs have the same overlap in beliefs. Her title of Ragana has been speculated to mean "clairvoyant, seeress", "with horns", "ghost, spirit" or "ruling goddess, queen". As Lauma she clothes and protects lost children. She may appear to you in your dreams. She is, of course, a spinning goddess. Her spiritual servants are called *laume*.

164

Ragana can appear as a young woman as well. In songs the names of Ragana and Žverūna are used interchangeably,[158] which shows that Ragana can be seen in her younger form as Devana/Žverūna, "The Beast Goddess". Ragana is described in the early spring as appearing near streams as a "beautiful nude woman combing her golden hair."[58] In these descriptions we see her seasonal transformation and her connection with the fey, since this sounds just like the descriptions of the lovely young *Rusalka*. She is freely sexual, which is later vilified and turned into tales of her "dominating men" and "exhausting them after a night's orgy".

Of course, Veliona may change her shape at will, including into a cat, pig, fish, bird, but her most common animal incarnation is the snake or the toad. The toad also has accumulated the symbolism of the vagina, womb, female sexuality and giving birth.[159] While both snakes and toads relate to fertility and prosperity. As Ragana she is recorded as transforming into a variety of birds such as a crow, a magpie, a swallow, or a quail but she is not limited to these.[58] She is said to transform into a fish, hedgehog, sow, mare, dog, moth or butterfly.

Veliona keeps the balance of nature, because unchecked growth is what causes cancer. She holds the power of the waxing and the waning of the moon, the sunrise and sunset, the cycle of growth and death and consequent rebirth. She knows the healing herbs and when necessary, the herbs that can cause abortion or an easy death. Thus the healing herb elecampane is named after her with Welenā being the oldest form of the name Helenē/Ellen (going back to Indo-European roots).[69] Veliona is the Mistress of the Animals both culling the herd and bringing forth baby animals. She embodies balance.

Followers: *laume, mavje, navja, ragana or raganius, rusalka, vila, wila, véščii vol'ga, volx*

Sacred Day, Time or Holiday: Saturdays & February 2nd (or Feb. 12th), Veija Noc (Great Night) from Winter Solstice to Spring Equinox.

Sacred Space: forests, wooded river banks, barn, pastures, places of commerce such as a market, low places, caves, underground springs, islands

Sacred Animals: bear, wolf, lynx, snake, dragon, dog, reptiles, especially the snake, fish, black birds (raven, crow), magpie, owl, quail, swallow, sow, mare, hedgehog, moth, butterfly

Sacred Plants: walnut tree, rowan tree, willow, cedar, holly, ivy, mistletoe, basil, woodland herbs, wormwood, autumn crocus (aka naked ladies), burdock, fungus, root plants (such as beets, turnips, etc.), elecampane, birch (especially the weeping birch)

Sacred Objects: a forked staff or a shepherd's staff, horns (ram, goat, or bull), black key, (gate of the Underworld,) flute (especially a *sopilka*), boat, ammonite fossil, broom

Offerings: bread, walnuts, mead or other sweet, heavy wine or fruit cordials, black fur, music, coins of precious metals, gems or raw ore, jet, obsidian, onyx, cedar incense

"Old Woman with a Distaff", 1710.

33. Urna z napisem.

34. Urna z ręką i kulczykiem.

Illustration by Henryk Biegeleisen circa 1900.
Slavic cinerary urns with Slavonic runes found in the
ancient grave of Poland in Lednogóra, Poland.
(Source: Wikimedia Commons, public domain)

Baba Yaga (BAH-bah YAGH-gah) - "Old Lady/Grandmother with Horns" or "Forest Mother" (Baba Gorbata, Baba-jaga, Baba Jedza, Baba Korizma, Baba Roga, Babaroga, Endzibaba, Holle, Indžibaba, Jazibaba, Jedza, Jedsi Baba, Jezi Baba, Jezibaba, Ježibaba, Jitnaya Baba, kvatma baba, kvatrnica, Pehra baba, Perchta, Poludnitsa, Pozhinalka, Požinalka, Prezpołnica, Pripolnica, Sumska Maika, Wjerbava, Worawy, Wurlavu, Yaga Baba, Yaga-Yagishna, Yegi Baba, Yeza, Yezinka, Yezli baba)

In Croatia she is known as Babaroga, which roughly translates to "Old Lady/Grandmother with Horns." Baba meaning an "old woman" or "grandmother."[160] It can mean "witch" or "hag" and is used to scare children into behaving.[161] Yaga means "anger" in Slovenia, while in Serbia it means "horror and shudder."[162] It's also particularly interesting that in Sanskrit *yaga* means "snake" or "serpent." Her name Jezibaba means "night-butterfly" (moth) which also carries the meaning of witch. She has also been compared to the Bulgarian *gorska majka*, which means "Forest Mother." Andreas Johns writes that "figurative meanings of b*aba iaga* include an old woman living alone, an untidy woman, or a human figure made of snow (in Russia usually called a "snow woman," *snezhnaia baba*), a female bear…"[163]

I believe that Baba Yaga is just another aspect of Siva/Diva in her winter, crone form. Her long hooked nose gives her away as the beaked Bird Goddess. She is essentially "Grandmother Winter" or another version of Mora. She can also be perceived as "Grandmother Snake" connecting her to the unconscious and our dormant kundalini energy.

The much maligned Baba Yaga becomes transformed back into the powerful crone aspect of the goddess when we weed through all the descriptions. Although she has been slandered terribly, we can see through the descriptions of how ugly she is and see her as a very powerful, older woman. Her cottage is described as standing "on fowls' legs"[6] and looking towards the forest, but when the hut is entreated nicely it will turn around the front of the house to the person addressing it. In this we can see the symbols of her as a death goddess, but it is a misunderstanding of her role as the Dark Mother who controls the regenerative energy of the world. Death leads to new life. The fallen log becomes the nurturer of fungi, home of critters, and eventually decays to dirt and provides the fertilizing force of the woodland floor. The wisdom of the cycle of birth, death and new life is hers. From her womb (symbolized by the oven or cave) comes rebirth. When life became linear and death was feared Baba Yaga was turned into a terrifying crone.

When Baba Yaga ventures out into the woods she is described as riding inside an iron mortar which she propels with the pestle, and as she goes she sweeps away the traces of her passage with a broom. In this symbolism she reveals her renewing nature; the mortar and grinding pestle was a common tool of the herbalist and healer. The broom is the symbol of the magic working witch. She can control spirits, control time and has fire-breathing horses just as Hors-Dazbog does.[16]

Baba Yaga is frequently described as domestically spinning. This connects back to being one of the goddesses of Fate. However, one also makes their own fate by working industriously, and the Servian version of Baba Yaga will "burn the distaffs of lazy spinners." The spindle is a tool of Baba Yaga's and of her devotees (witches.) Intention can be spun into the yarn or woven into the cloth. While Baba Yaga spins the elements of life into the child in the womb.

The symbol of the sieve connected to Mora's weather magic is connected to Baba Yaga as well. Although we don't see Baba Yaga riding in it, the sieve is included as one of the impossible tasks she sets for Vaselisa; to carry water in a sieve (which, because Vaselisa was kind, an animal helper shows her how to solve the problem by plastering the sieve with clay and moss.)

There has been mention of a more benevolent form of Baba Yaga in a tale where she is described as three sister "Baba Yagas" who are of a much more kindly nature and assist the hero of the story and give him good advice and magic presents. Even an Edwardian story collector living in an age before "Women's Lib" could understand the truth behind this aspect of the Triple Goddess, writing, "These [Baba Yagas] seem to be connected with the "Prophetesses," or "Wise Women," who were looked upon with so much honour in the old days of heathenism, and who became degraded into vulgar witches under the influence of Christianity."[6]

You can also see in Baba Yaga, Siva's healing powers and role as goddess of the witches. Ralston writes, "...often identical with the Baba Yaga is the *Vyed'ma*, or Witch. Her name, as well as that of the *Vyedun*, or Wizard, springs from the root *vyed*, whence *vyedat'*, "to know." In the old heathen times the *Vyed'ma* was the *Vyeshehaya zhena*, the wise or knowing woman, and was held in high reverence. As prophetess, poetess, medicine-woman, she exercised solemn functions; she was supposed to control the elements, to be able to compel the clouds to withhold or to pour forth rain, to prevent the sun from shining, or to gladden the earth with its rays."[6]

Baba Yaga is the ancient midwife, who can help you birth babies or projects. This is the reason the frog is sacred to her, not only is it a position one gets into to give birth (the embroidery pattern of a stylized mother giving birth is called "pretty frogs"), but the frog also transforms through all the stages of life[159] and that is Baba Yaga's province.

Baba Yaga is a powerful goddess. When she flies through the forest, the trees "writhe and howl as she passes." She harnesses the power of the storm and the whirlwind. When as "a black cloud" she chases fugitive heroes, she seems to be the thunder-cloud which threatens to blot out the light of day. It's a mistake to think that she does it out of cruelty. She is the natural consequence to your mistakes and you better remedy them. She is the family representative dealing out tough love. She is the justice bringer of the natural world. If we are lazy and selfish and don't limit our CO_2 pollution, Baba Yaga's power is in the just retribution of the tornados and savage storms. To work with Baba Yaga you must learn how to take care of our forests and earth, be respectful, and work hard, then she will reveal her magic to you.

Baba Yaga is a goddess that doesn't let you get away with being lazy or sloppy, because when you are working with the stronger forces of magic you need to be careful and wise. You are responsible for any results, intended or unintended!

Followers: *Babaroga, Vyeshehaya zhena, Vyed'ma* or *Vyadun, jezinka* (wood nymph), *jeze* (witch), *Baba*

Sacred Day, Time or Holiday: midnight, November 1st (All Souls/Halloween) March 1st (Baba Marta Day)

Sacred Space: crossroads

Sacred Animals: snake, cat, moth, butterfly (known as *babochka* in Russian, meaning "Old Woman), chickens, black sheep, magpie, mouse, shrew, mole, weasel, vixen, hedgehog, frog, toad, crab, pelican, turtle, mare, goat, bee.

Sacred Plants: sweet potatoes, root vegetables, hemp, cabbage, contorted hazelnut, elder trees, birch trees, spruce trees, medicinal herbs, yew tree, celery

Sacred Objects: cauldron, bones, mortar and pestle, dried chicken feet, besom (broom), twisted walking stick, magic staff, spindle, black yarn, sieve

Offerings: strong coffee, vodka, rum and other hard liquors, blood, dark chocolate, candies, cakes, sweets, black or grey wool and yarn, blackberries

"Baba Yaga" by I. Bilibin before 1930's

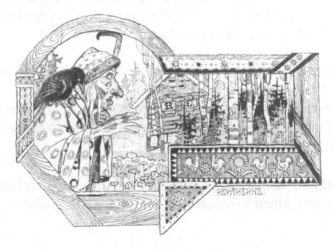

174

"Baba Yaga" by Nikolay A. Bogatov in Tales of the
Russian People, 1894.

Koshchei (KASH-sheh) "Old Grandfather Winter", "The Deathless" (Chuchilo, Chudo, Craciun, Karachun, Kaschei, Kaschtschei, Kashei, Kashel, Kashel-tsar' Bessmertnyi, Kerečun, Khursun, Kolschei, Korachun, Korchun Bessmortnyi, Korochun, Kosciej niesmiertelny, Koschuny, Kosh, Koshchai, Koshchei, Koshchei Bessmertnyi, Koshcheiushko, Koshel, Koshshui, Kostei, Kostii Bezdushnyi, Kostsei, Kot, Kot Bezsmertnyi, Kovshei, Kozel, Koz'olok, Kračun, Krakun, Mróz, Nij, Sitiwrat, Studenets, Treskun)

I know Baba Yaga is not normally pictured as having a male companion, but I assure you this is the case. Researcher Andreas Johns tells of a tale where "Baba Iaga and Kashchei appear as a fearsome couple who kidnaps a princess and freeze her. Kashchei breathes on a prince and his companies and turns them to stone, climbs in Baba Iaga's mortar with her, and kills the princess' horse with the pestle. In a later fight, Kashchei takes Baba Iaga in his arms and flees."[164] From this we see the typical image of Baba Yaga with Kashchei as her partner. In a few tales they are described as brother and sister, just as Deva and Devac are siblings and lovers. Ralston's describes "Koshchei the Immortal," as a mythical representation of Winter, not even recognizing him as a god. His name is derived from the word *kost*, a bone, whence comes *okostenget*, to ossify, to make hard as a bone or a stone, a figurative expression for "to freeze."[6] But one of his variations of a name,

Korachun, is also the name for the "short day," the Winter Solstice. Literally *karačun* means "to die." The term of *koshchei* can be used for a thin or bony man, as well as someone who is a miser.[164] Just a bit different from our modern vision of Father Christmas who comes around the Winter Solstice, but Korachun/Koshchei is pictured with a long white beard. The sacred bread served at Christmas (the Winter Solstice) is also called the *korochun*. He is the harvest god that got personified into a "spirit of Winter" and diminished in the tales from a god to simply an evil giant.

In tales, Koshchei has the ability to bring darkness and to freeze people. Like Baba Yaga his house is surrounded by a fence with human heads on them, recalling his duties guiding the dead and giving them rest.   In some Slavic Spring Equinox celebrations an effigy named "Chuchilo" or "Chudo" is destroyed to make way for spring. Author Russell Zguta writes, "The religious overtones of this ceremony are obvious; the god of darkness and death, symbolizing Winter and represented here by the puppet [effigy], is physically annihilated to make way for spring, the harbinger of new life and plenty."[110]

In many of the tales, Koshchei's soul is kept in an egg and he is destroyed when the egg is destroyed. But I would say this is merely the very garbled telling of the cycle of the seasons. Koshchei Bessmertnyi means "without death." He is described as "Koshchei the

Deathless" or "The Immortal," yet in the tales he is often killed when the egg is found. I remember this tale from childhood from the Red Fairy Book and the egg is hidden inside a duck, which is inside a hare, inside a crystal chest, buried under a green oak tree, which is on an island Buyan (Buian) in the ocean. Now that you understand that he is the winter form of the Lord of the Radiant Light you see the symbolism of the egg being his rebirth into his youthful spring form (Jarilo, Lado, or Kresnik.) The crystal chest is the cold of winter, the duck and the hare are symbols of the spring goddess. The spring goddess is also seen as Koshchei's "captured princess" who has not yet been released into the world until his "death."

Besides being a skinny old man with a long white beard, he was also a shape-changer. He could take the form of a young man if he liked or change into a storm or tornado. He is the same as the Belarusian god of winter, Ziuzia. Researcher Leu Horosko writes, "Folk tradition depicts him as an ugly old man with a long grey beard. He went about clad in a white fur, bare-headed and bare-footed, having in his hand an iron staff or mace. When moved to anger he would strike the tree trunks in the forest with his staff, bring ice and snow, and causing the winter to cast a cold shroud over the land."[5]

The linguistic origins of several Slavic animal's names point to a connection with Korochun. Author, Edward Stankiewicz, cites several researchers' work that have variations of "great-grandfather" or "male ancestor" as names for the mouse, rat, scorpion, and cricket, as well as to the puffball mushroom.[162]

He will take the form of a snake or dragon and his spiritual servants are embodied sometimes as snakes. To these grass snakes you should give offerings such as eggs and milk. Koshchei is a god of Slavic shamans.

Followers: *Călușari, koshchei, or koshchci iadun*
Sacred Day, Time or Holiday: Winter Solstice, winter
Sacred Space: caves
Sacred Animals: snakes, dragons, bulls, horses, goats, woodpeckers, rats, mice, crickets
Sacred Plants: oak trees, celery, mushrooms (especially puffballs), turnips and rutabagas
Sacred Objects: quartz crystals, statues of snakes and dragons, bones, eggs, staff
Offerings: statues of snakes and dragons, snow globes, clear crystals, *kutya*, grain porridge, pancakes, circular cakes or donuts

"Baba Yaga Dances with Old Man" with bagpipes -
mid-18th century. Remember Veles plays bagpipes?

Illustration for "Tzarevich Petr and the Wizard" (Koshchei) Ivan Bilibin, 1912.

Striᖯog (STREE-boog) "Lord of Winds & Spirits", "Father of the Winds" - (Bagajos, Bangputtis, Bardoayts, Erishvorsh, Erisvorsh, Erivorsh, Gardehts, Gardeoldiis, Gardoaitis, Gardoyts, Nehoda, Niepogoda, Strib, Striba, Stribi, Stryba, Strybog, Stryboh, Strzybog, Szélatya, Szélkirály, Paśvist, Percloitus, Perdoite, Pochvist, Pochwistel, Pogvist, Pogwid, Pohvist, Poshvist, Posvist, Poxvist, Pozvizd, Varpulis, Vejo, Vėjopatis, Vichera, Wejdievs, Wejo-patis, Wejopatis, Wejpons)

Radosavljevich in chronicling the writings of the 12th century monk Nestor states that Stribog is "a hostile deity, god of storms or winds, the Greek AEolus."[77] In the Word of Igor's Armament, it was written, "Behold the winds, Stribog's grandchildren…"[165] Since the priests of the time complained about the elements being worshipped as gods, I first thought of Stribog as the personification of air. However, Cross, the interpreter of the The Russian Primary Chronicles has a different opinion stating, "Stribog is usually interpreted as the god of the whistling winds, he may be viewed more properly as a vegetation spirit."[166] Ralston cites the Journal of the Ministry of National Enlightenment" saying, "Stribog, the God of the Winds, is derived from a word *Stri* (the air, or a certain state of the atmosphere) and may still be recognized in various geographical designations, such as Stribog's Lake (Stribozhe Ozero,) etc."[6] Stribog's Lake makes more sense when you know that in Belarus, "Stryboh" is known as the god of water. Yet, in the "*Slove ab palku lharave*" he is described as the god of winds again.[5] In an old Polish book from 1885, "Strybog" is described as "the king of waters and winds."[4]

When a strong storm wind arose the ancient Slavs would kneel in reverence to the Lord of the Winds. Further names of the "Lord of the Winds" are Bardoayts, Gardoyts, Perdoyts and the variation of Bangputtis, which means "the wind that blows the waves". People gathering amber would pray to Bangputtis and call out his name three times.[53]

We also have Varpulis (Warpulis) Vėjopatis (Wejopatis) known in the Czech Republic, Slovakia, Lithuania and Croatia. He is said to accompany Perun and causes the wind and noise of the storm.[167] The Victorian author, Von Ulrich connects Warpulis with the word *warpas* meaning "bell."[28] Varpulis is equated with Erishvorsh, Erisvorsh, or Erivorsh. (Note the onomatopoeia of these titles.) These may be other names for Stribog. In Lithuania, the word *wtjis* or *wejas* means "wind,"[168] so Wejdievs, Wejo-patis, Wejopatis, Wejpons means "God of the Winds", or "Father of the Winds". This corresponds to the Vedic god, Vayu. Praetorius tells about a Prussian fisherman who had a wooden image of Wejopatis affixed to the mast of his ship. In stormy weather he would "lift up both his hands towards it". As Vejopatis, he is described in Bullfinch's Mythology as the "Father of the Winds" with a beard, wings and two faces. From a 17th century drawing we have Vejopatis depicted as a naked, clean shaven, dual-faced, winged god. He holds a fish in his left hand and what looks to be a striped drum (described as a "tool") in his right hand and a rooster on his head. [169]

We also see him in the chronicles of the Lithuanians. There he is called Gardeoldiis, Gardoaitis, Percloitus, Perdoite.[120] He is pictured as a giant winged being who presided over the winds and the sea. Fishermen would "offer sacrifices of fish to him, eating the remains of what they had offered, and drinking very freely: after which the priest, whom they called *Sigonotta*, took observations of the winds, and predicted to them the day and place on which they were to have successful fishing. He was represented by them as an angel of enormous bulk standing upon the waters, and turning the winds which ever way he pleased."[170] He was worshipped by sailors who feared in his anger he might overturn their ship.

Dlugosz calls Stribog, "Pogwid," writing, *"Poloni autem quaslibet vanas creaturas, solem lunam, auram quam Pogwid appellabant cultu divino prosequebantur."* Latin scholar, Anthony West translates Dlugosz's description as "The Poles moreover would lavishly attend with divine cult such vain creations as the sun, the moon, the air, which they used to call Pogwid."

The migratory birds called swifts are sacred to Stribog. They like to nest in chimneys, hollow trees and caves which connects to this god's chthonic nature. There are many magical caves in Slavic lands that are said to be the "home of the winds" or where the "Wind Brother lived".[171] Migratory fish such as carp, sturgeon and salmon would also be sacred to him and they can bring news to and from the Spirit World.

Just like Kresnik, Stribog can have wings and fly. He can also transform himself into a whirlwind (like Veles). Offerings can be given to him at whirlpools. If you are working with him, whirlpools also provide a place of power to work spells with his help. Call his name three times. Another way to connect with this deity would be with a conch seashell in which you can hear the sound of the wind and waves.

Followers: *płanetnik* and *płanetnika, sigonotta, stregoni*
Sacred Day, Time or Holiday: Twelve days between winter and spring
Sacred Space: towers, windy places, ocean, whirlpools
Sacred Animals: eagles, swifts, billy goats, stags, bulls, oxen, wolves, boars, rooster, fish (especially migratory fish)
Sacred Plants: hawthorn, oak

Sacred Objects: fish-shaped amulets, fish teeth, scales or bones, feathers, wind vane, amber, bell, seashells
Offerings: fish, cookies shaped as bulls, oxen, boars or stags

"Worship of Stribog" La Religion Ancienne et Moderne des Moscovites. 1698
This is probably a Christian propaganda illustration, rather than what a Pagan statue of "Stribi" actually looked like.

"Eurus, the God of the Winds" by James Stuart & Revett Nicholas, 1762.

Striga (STREEG-ah) "Goddess of Winds & Spirits", "Mother of the Winds", "Queen of the Witches" (Befana, Bercht, Behrta, Berchta, Berhta, Erche, Frau Bert, Frau Frie, Frau Gode, Frau Harke, Frau Herke, Frau Holl, Frau Selga, Freke, Gode, Guode, Gwode, Harke, Helche, Herche, Herke, Herkja, Holda, Holle, Hulle, Huldr, Kvaternica, Luca, Lucia, Lutzi, Luzie, Łucja, Pehta, Perahta, Perhta-Baba, Rupfa, Saelde, Selga, Selten, Stampa Strägerle, Sträggele, Stratim, Strega, Streggele, Striga Holda, Strigoi, Strix, Stryha, Strzyga, Szélanya, Veja Mat, Wejamaat, Werra, Zälti, Zlobna Pehta)

Most online sources will mention Stribog, as the God of the Winds. A revelation came to me in a dream, that Striga was the partner of Streibog. Once I went looking for her, I found information that backs up that the title of Striga existed; like "Striga Holda" and the Slavic vampiric spirits and witches known as *strigoi*. From her symbols we can see Striga is just another title of Mora, Morana, Marzana, Mara and Baba Yaga and like them she got reduced to a malicious vampiric spirit. Like Baba Yaga, "fraw Hulde" is described with a "tremendous nose",[172] like a hawk or bird of prey (this indicates that she is the Bird Goddess). She would seem connected to the Baltic Giltine who is also described as having a long nose and long tongue. Her title of Bercht means "the Bright One".

We see her in Serbia by the name of Stratim, described as the "assistant" of the god of wind, Stribog, for all that she is described as the mother of all the birds in the world. She is portrayed as having the body of a bird with the head and chest of a woman. The movement of her wings could create a huge wave in the sea, so sailors would give her offerings. So you can see the legends reflecting this goddess in her role as Bird Mother and Wind Mother. I believe these tales devolved into the Greek legends of the sirens and harpies, while in Russian lore the Goddess became transformed into the fantastical birds called Sirin, Alkonost, and Gamayun and in Persian (Iranian) lore, she became the healing bird, Simurgh and the oriental Phoenix. She is probably also the origin of the figures of Medusa. The astonishing variety comes from the fact that the oldest depictions of the Bird Goddess go back to the Paleolithic era about 30,000 years ago.[173]

Witches in Italy can be called *strega* or *streghe*, but that has accumulated a negative connotation, so they tend to use *mago* (for men) and women are called mag, *magara*, or *ma'ara*.[174] Hmmm... sound familiar? Poppy seeds were used to ward her away, yet these were probably offerings originally. She is hardly remembered in the Slavic lands, but we can trace her common origins through the surrounding countries and her beginnings were much gentler remembered as the gift-giving La Befana of Italy or Mother Holle of Germany.

In Hungary, we have Szélanya meaning the "Wind Mother".[175] She is the goddess of winter storms and the wild winds of winter. She takes care of the souls and rebirth. However, she's also connected to water: wells, the watery Underworld and the waters of birth. She is the mistress of wild things.

It is thought that her name of Striga became transformed into the Norse Friga,[176] which would make Friga her winter form and Freya her summer form in Norse lore. In the same way, this goddess would transform into Devana (the Maiden) in the spring, which is why the Italian *strega* (witches) are said to worship the goddess Diana.[172] In Germany, her young form would seem to be Perchta.

Striga is a form of the Bird Goddess. Her followers sometimes wore a beaked mask to connect with her at Carnival and in tales Berhte/Perchta reputedly had a goose foot or swan foot. The name of *strigoi* linguistically connects to the Latin name for owls which is *Strix*.

She is usually depicted as elderly with disheveled hair (Slavic witches are always described as working magic with their hair down and loose.) She is sometimes described as crowned, such as the holly crown of her youthful form as Lucia or a more regal crown as a queen. Of course, she changes her shape from old to young, or appears as a bird of prey, a wolf, a goat, a donkey, or with a horse's head. Her followers at the liminal festival between seasons may wear masks with horns (or a beak), as well as fur cloaks and hats.

Like her partner, Streibog, Lord of the Winds, Striga would seem to control the weather as her counterpart Frau Holle is known to create falling snow when she shakes out her feather blankets. She causes thunder when she shakes her keys and controls the clouds and fog. As Frau Holle is also said to lead the Wild Hunt; a gathering up of souls in the wild winds of winter. She is sometimes pictured mounted on a horse. This hunt is also said to increase the fertility of the land. In Slovene folklore we see the wild hunt with the spirits, the *divja jaga* being led by Pehtra (aka Mora/Baba Yaga/Striga) in the twelve days between the Winter Solstice and New Years.

Striga's witches were thought to fly in the wild winds over Babia Gora on the border of Poland and Slovakia and land in the Haleczkowa fields. They are said to bring magical herbs and flowers and sing, dance, feast and make magic. Folk tales report they transformed poor peasant lads into horses and rode them to this gathering[177] (sounding much like the folk tales of fairies in Ireland). The twelve days after this were thought to predict the weather for the following twelve months. I believe the original dates would have been starting at the Winter Solstice and going for twelve days. Although this same twelve day wild period can also be celebrated "before Lent", as the *Perchten* of Lienz, Austria do[172] (so perhaps around the Spring Equinox or the "new year" at May Day). Indeed, we find in Switzerland the festival of *Streggelejagen* with scary creatures called *Streggele*, running around at Easter.

In tales she gives virtuous girls luck and those who are lazy are punished. I suspect her earlier nature is reflected in the traditions of Lautenthal, Germany where she takes the "naughty" into her home in the forest and reshapes them into "better beings". This would be more in keeping with her role as Queen of the Witches to take those "wild women" who do not fit the norm and she trains them. The mastery of magic requires the mastery of the self, thus they would emerge as "better beings". Motz writes, "...we know that the adjective [wild] had a meaning, almost lost in our time, of 'belonging to the forest.'"[172] Thus Striga resides in woods, caves, wells and wild places. She has an educational role and may be looked to as a tough but fair teacher. Striga is undoubtedly an initiator of shamanic witches since in tales, all her counterparts (Holde, Perchta, Luzie) are said to "punish" girls by splitting them open and filling them with rocks or other natural materials. Motz puts forth the theory that this refers to the process in shamanic initiation known as "dismemberment" and I totally agree.

Black and white birds tend to symbolize the goddess who transforms from Summer to Winter. The swift is sacred to Stribog and presumably Striga. The chthonic character of this bird is that it calls at night, nests in caves and disappears in winter (thought to travel to the spirit world).

Followers: *skazki, strzyga, strega* or *strigo*i
Sacred Day, Time or Holiday: night of December 12th (St. Lucy's Day), Winter Solstice (about December 21st) and the twelve following days (to about January 6th), New Year's Day, January 6th, Spring Equinox (*Strinenija*)
Sacred Space: caves, underground, in a well, in the mountain or forest
Sacred Animals: owls, geese, swans, snakes, cats, dogs, wolves, frogs, toads, swifts, pigs, horses
Sacred Plants: poppy seeds, basil, walnuts, verbena
Sacred Objects: silver, three candles to represent the triple goddess, wooden spoon, keys, broom
Offerings: silver coins or other silver objects, dumplings, eggs, herring or carp, milk, fried cakes, grain porridge with honey, candles, "S" shaped buns with raisin eyes to represent snakes, poppy seeds, poppy seed cakes, Strega liqueur, figs, dates
Symbol: a zig-zag "S"

"Berchta and her Train" from the book Making of America, 1873.

Zozim - (zah-ZEEM) "The Buzzing One" "The Joyful God" (Auxtejas Wissagistis, Babil, Babilas, Babilo, Babilos, Babylon, Bes, Bibčių Bobelis, Bičbirbis, Biczbirbins, Birbulis, Birbus, Bubil, Bubila, Bubilas, Bubili, Bubilo, Bubilos, Bublos, Bybulus, Prokorimos, Raguto, Ragutis, Trimpus, Zosim) -

Zozim is worshiped as a god of apiculture, bees, wax, mead, revelry, and bawdy songs (and possibly a card-playing water spirit). I have found mentions of him in the Czech Republic, Ukraine and Russia. While in Prussia, Latvia and Lithuania he is called Babilas. [36] He is the patron of the alcoholic honey drink *medovukha* which evolved into mead-making. Zozim is a joyful, fertile, sexual, reveling god (although he's somewhat older and somewhat more portly).

The god Zozim would have been very important at one time because the production of wild honey was the first major exports of the Slavs. His role of god of beekeepers was taken over in the Middle Ages by the similarly named St. Zosima, the patron saint of bees. St. Zosima has April 30th as his feast day, which shows up in the Pagan sacrifice of tossing a bee comb in a millstream at midnight of May Day Eve to ensure a plentiful harvest of honey.[6] In the lore of St. Zosima he has the power of foretelling as well as healing. It may well be that Zozim's followers used alcohol or poppy to get into an altered mind-state for shamanic traveling and foretelling. I believe the reason Zozim was associated with playing cards was

195

because it was considered a game of chance. Since all things are connected a game of chance could be used to understand the underlying plan of the Divine. Thus playing cards were used for foretelling purposes in the manner of Tarot cards today.

Biczbirbins/Babilas is the same god as Zozim; both names have an onomatopoeic origin. Zozim as the "Bee God" is one of the "faces" of the joyful fertility god, Seibog. The beekeeping season fell between April 30th (May Day Eve) to October 2nd/10th,[178] which happens to be the feast days of St. Zosimus and St. Savvaty (Sabbatius.) This probably connects to the Thracian (Bulgarian) grain god, Sabazius (Sabazios.) Interesting enough, while one form of his name, "Biczbirbins," sounds like a bee buzzing and in Lithuanian *burbti* means "humming," another Lithuanian variation is *burbulas* which means "water bubble," or "whirlpool." Zozim is connected to the water spirits, the *vodyanoy*. There is a description given by Ralston of the *vodyanoy* as "a naked old man, with a great paunch and a bloated face. He is much given to drinking, and delights in carouses and card-playing. He is a patron of beekeeping..."[6]

Auseklis/Ūsiņš is definitively the younger version of this god, while Zozim seems to have the qualities of the older god. Notice how Ūzinš also has a buzzy sound like Zozim. Professor William Morrison describes "Babilas" with a little more censure, as "a corpulent, gluttonous, over-sexed, hairy, buzzing

196

spirit whose model may have been the drone bee."[179]

Zozim also had a love of physical pleasure; enjoying sex, music, good food and alcoholic drink. Yet he wanted his followers to have that as well and blesses them with good health, sexual pleasure, joyful inebriation and delicious foods.

Followers: could be *guslarz* or *guslarka* (a shamanic practitioner) and the lesser water spirits, the *vodenoy*
Sacred Day, Time or Holiday: Tuesdays, February 2nd, 10th, 11th or 14th, March 16th or the Spring Equinox, May Day Eve and May Day (April 30th, May 1st/6th), August, especially August 1st & 2nd, between October 2nd & 10th and October 27th (the Gate of Winter.)
Sacred Space: near a beehive, meadows, millpond, streams
Sacred Animals: bee, bull
Sacred Plants: clover, linden trees, meadow flowers, poppies, fruit trees, vines, ivy, grapes
Sacred Objects: amber, beehive, beeswax, flute, chalice, shot glass, phallic shapes, playing cards, dice, Tarot (all forms of divination)
Offerings: fresh water, honeycomb, *pysanky*, beeswax candle, tobacco, alcoholic drinks (especially mead and *medovukha*), bread, peas and honey, poppy seeds, bee pollen, royal jelly, amethyst, *buben* (tambourine), gingerbread

"Vodyanoy" V. Malyshev, 1910.

Ziza - (ZI-zah) "The Shining Goddess" "The Goddess of Abundance" (Cisa, Ctitel, Cyca, Czciciel, Dzydzilelya, Zizila, Zizilia, Zyza, Zyzila, Zyzilia)

In Hebrew Ziza means "splendor", "shining" or "abundance". While in Slavonic lore she is remembered as the goddess of love and sexuality. She is paired with Didilia. Didilia is the goddess of childbirth and babies. Since they are a paired goddess, there is the possibility that Didilia is the young spring goddess, while Zizilia would be the older goddess. Other variations of her name connect to names of the planet Venus. Which may make Didilia as the Morning Star and Zizilia as the Evening Star.

Ziza is another title for Siva, so I see no need to repeat the information.

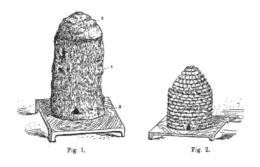

"Romanian beehives" by Frédéric Damé, 1898.

Koliada - (koh-lee-AH-dah) "Maiden of Midwinter" (Ciotia, Colindă, Colleda, Kaleda, Kalèda, Kalëdienë, Kalėdos, Kaliada, Kalyada, Kòlãda, Koleda, Kolędowanie, Koledsa, Kolenda, Koliada, Kolinda, Koljada, Koljadu, Kolyada, Kolyadka, Žyva-Hramavica)

While English researchers erroneously recorded that Kaleda, or Koliada, was the "god of peace,"[18] Koliada would seem to be a name used for the goddess, that stems from the name of the mid-winter holiday. In Bulgaria, the Winter Solstice is "Koleda" which comes from the verb *kolya*, meaning "to slaughter" because a pig is traditionally sacrificed at this time. The pig is sacred to the Mother Goddess.

Originally the "new year" was celebrated in the spring, but the calendar has been rearranged many times. At one point the "new year" was on the same day as the Winter Solstice. Then Christmas got put on the Winter Solstice which by this point was accidentally celebrated on December 25th, instead of the longest day of the year, December 20/21 (and to further complicate things in the old Julian calendar it would be January 6th). So when the celebration of the young spring goddess got shifted to the winter she picked up the title of the holiday, Koliada. She is a joyful personality in the midst of bitter winter. She could be pictured as a young child or a radiant young maiden reborn on the Winter Solstice.

200

Koliada is the early springtime aspect of the goddess Siva, with her male partner, Kolyado/Seibog/Dazbog. A Victorian chronicler, Hector Munro wrote, "Kolyada, a beneficent spirit who was supposed to visit the farms and villages in mid-winter and bring fertility to the pent-in herds and frost-bound seeds. The festival in honour of Kolyada was held about the 25th of December, the date when the Sun was supposed to triumph over the death in which Nature had gripped him and to enter on his new span of life."[180]

In Belarus, "Kaliada" was known to be another name for Žyva (Siva). She could also go by the name of Ciotia or Hramavica.[5] She was recorded as the "mother" of Dažboh, the young sun god that vanquished winter, but we've seen where they are partners of each other. Siva's symbol is a goat with golden horns, which is usually included in the Winter Solstice (Christmas) processions.

Koliada is celebrated at the Winter Solstice festival named in her brother-husband's honor. The young Lord of Radiant Light is renewed and growing stronger each day. The spring carnival that was celebrated at the re-birth of young Jarilo or Kresnik are moved to the Winter Solstice and the image of a Sun (or Star) is paraded around the village. In the celebration of this holiday, a man crossdresses (like the ancient priest/esses of old) and plays the part of the Goddess. They are called "Bride" and they carry a distaff and spin in these holiday processions.

Fresh water from a spring or well is drawn on the morning of the Winter solstice. An offering of basil is given to the goddess at this time. This should be the first water drawn from the well at dawn. This holds special energy and can be kept for healing purposes, although some is used to bake a ritual cake. The grain is used from the last sheaf harvested. This holy joining of the powers of the god and goddess is shared among family members. Pieces are ritually broken off, rather than cut, so that energetically it is still connected and connects the family.

Followers: *koledari*
Sacred Day, Time or Holiday: Winter Solstice, December 21st
Sacred Space: near water
Sacred Animals: sow
Sacred Plants: basil
Sacred Objects: sun or star symbols, candles
Offerings: spring water, honey

"A man presenting a goat at a Malanka ceremony" in Belarus by Michał Elwiro Andriolli, 1887
Malanka is a Christianized holiday that incorporates Pagan traditions celebrated at the "new year".

Koliado - (koh-lee-AH-doh) "Youth of Midwinter" (Boshizh, Bozhik, Božic, Bozvicv, Bystizyc, Govsen, Koleda, Koledo, Koliodka, Kolyado, Ovsen, Ovsenj, Radimicu, Tausen)

His name is sometimes written with the feminine ending of Koliada, yet they are referring to the male deity. The boar is sacred to him because it is usually eaten on New Year's Day (which would have been the Winter Solstice.)[181] In the older Slavic traditions, he was a youth of spring and used to be celebrated on March 1st, The Feast of Ovsen (which was probably attached to the Spring Equinox.) But when the celebration of New Year's changed to the winter, his songs were sung on December, 31st, New Year's Eve,[6] but should rightfully be on the Eve of the Winter Solstice. His name of Ovsen is believed to come from oves, meaning "oats," showing he is a bountiful provider, the young Radiant Lord of Light.

He is the successor to the old Badnjak, the old Lord of Light, just as Svarozich is the young form of Svarog (just other ways of perceiving the Lord of Radiant Light.) Eventually this evolved into our concept of the Old Man New Year and the Baby New Year.

Ralston records one of Koliado's rituals, where young boys go from house to house, scattering grain of different kinds, but mainly oats and singing:

"In the forest, in the pine-forest,
There stood a pine-tree,
Green and shaggy.
        Oh, Ovsen! Oh, Ovsen!
The Boyars came,
Cut down the pine,
Sawed it into planks,
Built a bridge,
Covered it with cloth,
Fastened it with nails.
        Oh, Ovsen! Oh, Ovsen!
Who, who will go
Along that bridge?
Ovsen will go there,
And the New Year,
        Oh, Ovsen! Oh, Ovsen!"

Another song asks:
"On what will he come?
On a dusky swine.
What will he chase?
A brisk little pig."[6]

In a foretelling ritual for the new year (which you could do on the New Year or more correctly on the Winter Solstice), two youths are dressed up. As Ralston relates, "One of them, called the Rich Kolyada, is dressed in new and holiday attire, and wears on his head a wreath made of ears of rye; the other, whom they call the Poor Kolyada, wears a ragged suit and a wreath made of threshed-out straw. When they come to a cottage they wrap up each of the two youths in long coverings, and tell the owner of the house to choose one of them. If his choice falls upon the Rich Kolyada, a song is sung by his visitors, which states that a good harvest awaits him, and plenty of money; but if he chooses the Poor Kolyada, then the singers warn him that he must expect poverty…" In this we see "Kolyado," depicted as a handsome youth with a crown of grain. [6]

Researcher, Nikola Milošević, writes that "Koledo gave people the knowledge of the universe and the celestial bodies. He gave them a book about the stars that the Slavs called Koledo's Star Book."[109] Milošević explains that the Greeks said they got their knowledge of the zodiac and the stars from the "Hyperboreans from the north." According to the Greeks the Hyperboreans "never waged wars" and worshipped solar deities. The Greeks may have been referring to the Slavs. Indeed, many of these Slavic deities do match up with astrological symbols and stars: Devana with the Great Bear (Big Dipper), the "Pole Star" as the celestial connection to the trunk of the Tree of Life, Siva's "Bird Way (the Milky Way), Jarilo and Mars, Jarila and Venus, etc. Plus, wintertime is the perfect time to really observe the night sky, with long cold and clear nights.

Followers: *koledari*

Sacred Day, Time or Holiday: Winter Solstice, December 21st
Sacred Space: hills
Sacred Animals: boar, mink
Sacred Plants: grain, oats, rosemary
Sacred Objects: boar tusk, sun and star symbols, candles, lanterns decorated with rosemary
Offerings: grain, coins, wine, pork, rosemary

"Belarusian Carolers of Gorki district" 1903.

Mokosh, Berehynia seem to incorporate all the seasonal components of the Triple Goddess.

Triglava and Triglav represent all three phases of the Goddess and God together, as do Rozhanitsa and Rod.

"Triglaw" one of the Prillwitz idols discovered in 1896. Its authenticity is still in doubt.

ꟿokosh (MOH-kosh) "Mother of the Harvest"
"Mother of Good Fortune" "Mother of Happiness" (Baba, Baba Keslaugubaia, Macosch, Macosh, Macosha, Macosk, Makoc, Ma Kosh, Makos, Makoša, Maksh, Makus, Matoha, Matoga, Moccas, Mococize, Mogosch, Mokocize, Mokosha, Mokoš, Mokos, Mokosi, Mokošica, Mokoshi, Moksha, Mokush, Mokusha, Mokushkha, Mokysha, Moskasla, Moško, Muggish, Mukes, Mukus, Muuks, Parascabeah, Parasceve, Parascheva, Paraschiva, Paraska, Paraskeva, Paraskevi, Petka, Piatnitsa, Pjatnica, Prascovia, Pyatnitsa, Pyatnitsa Proscovia, Vela, Vila, Vukoša, Wchossa.)

There are many conflicting sources for the origin of Mokosh's name. Linguist Trstenjak identifies her name as coming from Old Russian.[25] While Margaret Merisante cites Johanna Hubbs' theory that Makosh is from the Finno-Ugric goddess named Moksha.[182] The Encyclopedia of Ukraine records that her name "is derived from the word combination *maty kota* 'mother of the cat,' that is, 'mother of good fortune.'"[35] According to linguist Max Vasmer, Mokosh's name is derived from the same root as Slavic words *mokry*, 'wet', and *moknut(i),* 'get wet'. [183] She is also known as "Mother Friday."

At first Mokosh looked like she didn't fit the usual pattern, but then I found in Slovenian lore that the winter goddess Mora and "Makurška" trade places in the year. As Boris Čok wrote, "It is difficult to ignore the linguistic similarity between Mokoška and Makurška, or [researcher] Šmitek's hypothetical connection between Deva and Mokoš."[78] Mokosh sort of blends the primal earth energy of Mat Zemla and the "living water"/healing powers of Siva/Deva in her maternal, summer form. She is certainly connected to the Bird Goddess since she is supposed to fly in the shape of a bird.

Like Siva, Mokosh is associated with water, wells, marshes and the earth. From a manuscript written about 1113, the Primary Chronicle, some short descriptions were recorded of the representations of deities that Vladamir the Great erected back when he was still Pagan. It names several gods and one goddess who is described as, "Mokosha, whom sorceresses and *zhrytsi* (priestesses) came to worship."[184] Women go to Mokosh for healing and inner transformation. She is also seen as a goddess of wealth and abundance.

She is a patron of the "womanly arts"; the goddess of spinning, weaving, laundering, embroidery, sheep and shearing. (Keep in mind that flax has to be soaked in water in order to get the fibers out.) Some sources state that she was the goddess of music as well (like Siva.) Her color is the rich red of life's blood. As earth mother, Mokosh takes back the soul at death (since the dead were buried in the earth or their ashes returned to it.) In Belarus, "Makoša" is only vaguely remembered and thought to be "the patroness of sheep-shearing and spinning"[5] and as such, a lock of wool was dedicated to her at the shearing.

Like we've seen in Siva's lore, Mokosh is connected to water, music, and healing. Since the rain brings fertile life energy to the earth, it is sometimes referred to as "Mokos' milk."[185] Siva was always associated with magical powers, both from her foretelling abilities and magical healing abilities. Mokosh incorporated this and is perceived as being the "weaver of one's fate." Since witches sometimes "meddle" with this, they work along with Mokosh. In 16th century Russia female magic workers were called *mokose*. However, her association with fertility and sex also brought the interpretation to the Russian word *mokosja* meaning "a woman of easy virtue,"[186] since the Christian viewpoint brought shame to this natural, joyous function.

Modern researcher, Jelka Vince Pallua, has made some recent connections regarding Mokosh with large stones in Croatia. These large stones were associated with wells, water or being moist and wet. There was also passed down the tradition of kissing the Baba when you first passed them, as well as leaving offerings of fruit or wheat. These "Babas" were located at borders of towns, and in the town of Grobnik she is located near the entrance to the town, thus giving her the title of **"Mistress at the Gates."**[186] She stands at the liminal spaces:

211

borders, doorways, between Summer and Winter and between our world and the Underworld.

It is recorded in the Encyclopedia of Goddesses and Heroines that "as late as the sixteenth century, Christian chronicles complained that Slavic women still 'went to Mokosh' for she was preeminently a woman's divinity."[185] The word *motok* is another word for spindle or spinning wheel, with which she shares her name.[19] The imagery of spinning is often connected to life in general and mothers in particular. A child forming in the mother's womb is envisioned as unspun wool that forms as yarn on the spindle, while the mother is the distaff or basket of wool that forms the child out of its own essence. Thus the Slavic riddle recorded by scholar Mirjam Mencej, "The mother shrinks, the child grows. What is it? Spinning."[187] While the mother's essence is connected to the spirit world and all of her foremothers. With our current knowledge of science we could even equate that imagery to our DNA. Thus Mokosh is directly related to the thread of a person's fate. We see the connection in linguistics, where cognate words "refer both to spinning, yarn and cloth to fate, luck and wealth."[188] Like Siva with her connection to the Fates, Mokosh, combined with Dolya and Nedolya are also seen as a manifestation of the Fates.

We can see Mokosh's origins connecting back to this loving aspect of the goddess Siva. Mokosh gives us a more motherly way to connect to the Goddess. She is also implored to by young maidens as a patroness of marriage. In Privlaka, Croatia, young brides would bring an offering of apples and cakes to the village well in the morning after they were married.[189]

In Russia, the goddess was demoted to the realm of a house-spirit that only came out at night to spin. She was further caricaturized by having a large head and long arms. Sometimes known as a house-spirit called Domosherika who lived behind the stove and predicted death in the family by crying.[190]

And to further solidify that Mokosh is just another form of the Mother Goddess, Researcher, Vesna Kakasevski, writes, "Mokos is sometimes identified with Vida, Svarog's wife. She was, along with Svarog, the creator of mankind..."[191]

Followers: *mokose* or *zhrytsi*
Sacred Day, Time or Holiday: Wednesday & Friday, New Moons, Mokosh's Day is the Friday that falls between October 25 to November 1, (St. Paraskevia's feast day is October 14th, or alternately October 26th.) Spring Equinox, Summer Solstice and the number 9 for the months of gestation
Sacred Space: home, hearth, barn, pastures, wooded hills, the cool, dark waters of wells, lakes and marshes

Sacred Animals: cat, mouse, rat, bird, bee, snake, cows

Sacred Plants: elder, willow, hemp, flax, rosemary, basil, apple, linden

Sacred Objects: red (the color of life's blood), spindle, distaff, spinning wheel, wool, flax fibers, hemp yarn, embroidery thread, shears, wooden spoon

Offerings: bee pollen, honey, bread, cake, milk, homemade cheese, fiber, fabric (especially handwoven), beads, a lock of your hair, vegetables, fruits of the harvest (especially apples), lock of wool, herbs

Symbol: "Y" shape

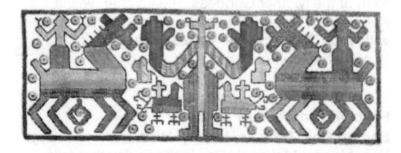

Russian Mokosh pattern with Kaluga embroidery
from the Belgorod Museum of Folk Culture.

"Dancing Mokosh" on the crown of Konstantinos IX,
National Museum of Hungary, Budapest. Estimated
year of creation 1042.
photo by Johnbod   (Creative Commons Attribution-
Share Alike license)

Berehynia (berh-HI-nyah) "The Goddess"

"The Protecting Mother Goddess" "Hostess Who Brings Mist and Covers Plants with Dew" (Beregina, Bereginia, Bereginin, Bereginya, Berehinia, Berehynja, Berehynyam, Beryhynia, Bogoroditsa, Bohynja, Mikko, Perehinia, Peregynia, Peregynya, Pergenia, Perginia, Pergynia, Perynia, Pokrov, Pokrova, Przeginia, Przeginie)

Berehynia is connected to Mokosh, since Mokosh was considered the protector of women and children. It is thought that the name Berehynia comes from the word *berech* meaning "to protect."[190] But *Bohynja* may simply mean "Goddess," representing the Mother Goddess in all her forms. Other interpretations tie her name "Beregina" to *bereg*, meaning shore or perhaps *berech*, meaning to protect.[192] The word *peregynya* is used to designate "a sacred oak forest growing on a hill."[23]

Pavlo Markovyc describes a standard anthropomorphized *pysanky* design used to represent the "mother goddess, the 'pagan' Great Goddess, or as she was also called: the Goddess Mokos, the Goddess Berehynja, and the Goddess Zyva. She always symbolized life and fertility and was worshiped as the mother of all living things."[193] Another name for her is "Bogoroditsa" which means "Birthgiver of God."[194] The different names including "Goddess" (Bohynja) and

216

"Queen" (Knjahynja) given to the same design on *pysanky* would seem to indicate that they are all the same goddess. The similarity of her name to the Phrygian goddess Berecyntia aka Cybele suggests a connection between Berehynia and Kurecija (who is also known as Cybele).

Her name variation of Peregynia is understood to be the **"Mother of the Thunderbolt"**. Various sacred hills are named after her such as the Holy Mountain Pergynia in Gołonóg now Dąbrowa Górnicza, Poland. [195] *Dąbrowa* comes from the Polish word *dąb* meaning "oak". This holy mountain now has a church built on top, but probably had a sacred oak grove before that.

However, I will record the lore associated with the name of Berehynia here, as it has come down today. Berehynia's holy day became subsumed by the Orthodox celebration of the Protection of the Theotokos (Mother of God) or Feast of the Holy Protectress on October 1st in the old calendar, now on the Julian calendar October 15th and in the Greek Orthodox Church it is celebrated on October 28th, which just so happens to be the day recorded as the feast day of the goddess Mokosh.[185] Or *most* accurately Mokosh's Day is the Friday that falls before November 1st. This is a day of rest and no one should sew, spin, or weave; this invokes the sympathetic magic that the winter will be a peaceful, easy time. St. Ursula's Day on October 21st, or the gates of winter (October 26 or October 31st) is mentioned as being sacred to Devana, Mokosh, and Berehynia. So we know they are the Bear Goddess (*Ursa* meaning "bear".) They are all just slightly different ways to view the protective Mother Goddess.

The word *pokrov* means both "veil/covering" and "protection"[194] and is another variation of this goddess' name. It is said Berehynia as "Pokrova" "divides the time into two," separating the active farming and herding time of year. After this date, the fields should be left fallow for the winter season. This time is marked by the Christian holidays of St. Demetrius and the Feast of the Holy Protectress. Since St. Demetrius is always depicted with a dark horse, I see these as the god and goddess of the "black" time of the year. Trading places with their "white role" on the May 6th feast of St. George who undoubtedly represents Jarilo paired with Jarila. Pokrova's Festival is essentially the same as that of Mikko's Day, also called Mikkeli or "Ram's Day" or the "gate of winter."[196] This Finnish holiday celebration has been documented back to the 5th century, and has the same connections to St. Demetrius's holiday, although it's named after St. Michael (who is also a horseman who fought a dragon, just like St. George.) The old date of St. Mikko's Day was October 12th; signaling the end of the harvest, predicting the weather rituals, the beginning of winter nights, etc.[196]

218

St. Michael is also a protector against "the dark of night." His feast day was moved from this two-part division of the year to the four part division where he is celebrated on the Autumn Equinox. His holiday is celebrated by most of Europe under the name of Michaelmas. In Celtic tradition, all financial accounts must be settled on this autumnal date. This is identical to the Serbian tradition of settling accounts on the date of St. Demetrius' Day. And just like the Serbians have a tradition of baking a special bread, the Celts bake a "Michaelmas Bannock" which was made by the oldest daughter without using any metal implements.[197] It is clearly a sacred ritual since any leftover flour had to be gathered up and sprinkled on the livestock as a protective blessing. There was also a blessing said over it that mentioned St. Michael and the Trinity.

The *pysanky* eggs decorated with the design named *"berehynia"* are interestingly enough, depicted with arms uplifted, but can have one, two or three pairs of arms,[198] attesting to her single, double or triple nature. She is sometimes even abstracted into a Tree-of-life design with pairs of flowers or leaves that mimic the arm positions. The designs on the *pysanky* tell us a lot. Sometimes in her three-armed "Berehynia" form she is given a crown as the "Queen of Life." Other times the crown is put on a curved swan shape that has a "wing" with three feathers and a spread tail. Even more interesting is a *pysanky* design called a *zmiya* (snake) symbol with the three-feathered wings. The *pysanky* lore keeps alive the description of "Berehynia" having the power over life and death.[198] Her form on *pysanky* as the "Tree of Life" design connects her back to Lada who is mentioned by Dagmara Dziekan in a paper cut design named *leluja* which depicts a "Tree of Life" flanked by two birds or roosters.[34] You can see that the Celtic concept of the Triple Goddess of Maiden, Mother, Crone was also shared by the Slavs and may have originated with them (since the Celts have lost the concept of the seasonal component of Spring, Summer and Late Autumn/Winter.) She is a patroness of marriage and family life.

As the god and goddess, her god partner's lore was also carried on as St. Andrew (Andrei) who supposedly had a vision of "Pokrova" (Mary, Mother of God) spreading her protective veil over all. The god and goddess of fertility transformed to the "patron saints" of marriage. Sometimes Christians would pray to "Father Pokrov" as the protective father, sometimes they would implore "Paraskeva Pyatnitsa." This combination of Paraskeva (Mokosh) and Pyatnitsa (Berehynia) show that these goddesses are essentially the same.

Looking at icons of "Pokrova" you will see the *orens* position of the arms, elbows bent and hands uplifted, sometimes holding a piece of cloth as she bestows her protective veil. This position is seen over and over again with the Mother Goddess; in Medieval

Russian temple rings worn as protective jewelry, in Slavic Iron Age sculptures protecting the home, going back even as far as Neolithic wall reliefs in Çatalhöyük, Turkey.

A sacred spot to her is Holy Jawir Hill, where there is a sacred well and a church to the "Protection of the Holy Mother of God". This is in Wysowa, Poland. The *jawir* is a sycamore maple that in lore was said to exist at the beginning of the world; the Tree of Life.

In the Orthodox church, the goddess, "Pokrova" was turned into the "Virgin of the Veil." Often depicted above the doors of the Christian church sanctuary with angels spreading the edges of her protective veil over all.[155] In more violent times, the Russians took this image and used it to protect the warriors of Novgorod, but I can't see where this goddess would "take sides." She is a goddess of life and protector of life… all life.

I couldn't figure out who her god partner was until I read the book Perun: The God of Thunder by Yoffe & Krafczik, who mentioned the similarity in names between *beregynia* and the Old Church Slavonic pregynia, the Polish *przeginia* and Old Russian *peregynia*.[107] The worship of the Tree of Life in the form of the oak and in holy oak groves called **pergyni* point to her being the Mother of Life with her consort of Perun. While Yoffe & Krafczik didn't make the connection back to this goddess, a quick examination of the root of *gyne* leads us to the Proto-Indo-European root of **gwen-* meaning woman, the Old English *cwen* meaning "queen" and the Sanskrit word *janis* meaning "a woman" and *gná* meaning "a goddess."[199] The PIE root **pere-* means "to produce." While Perun's name is usually thought to originate with the PIE word *perk* meaning "to strike". It may be that both have a common origin since lightning strikes were thought to increase the fertility of the land. Hopefully a linguist can pursue these interesting clues.

Followers: *Beregini, Bereginis, Bereginy* used for both her fairy servants and mortal shamanic women
Sacred Day, Time or Holiday: The Friday before November 1st (but sometimes celebrated on October 1st, October 14th or 15th or October 27th or 28th)
Sacred Space: home, near water and holy springs
Sacred Animals: goose, snakes, frogs
Sacred Plants: lavender, sycamore maple, oak
Sacred Objects: cloth or veil,
Offerings: lavender, goose, embroidered cloths
Symbol: on embroidery it is a women with her hands upraised

"Berehynia Pysanka" by Lubap, 2009   (Creative
Commons Attribution-Share Alike license)

"Berehynia" spreading her protective cloak. From the Slovene Ethnographic Museum in Ljubljana, Slovenia. Photo by author, 2018.

Triglav (TRIG-lahv) "The Three-Headed God"-

(Traian, Trajan, Trdoglav, Tribog, Tribogov, Trigelao, Triglas, Trigelaus, Trigelawo, Trigelawus, Trigelywus, Triglau, Triglaous, Triglaus, Triglous, Triglav, Triglava, Triglavu, Triglaw, Trihlav, Troglov, Troian, Troyan, Trygelawus, Tryglav, Trygław, Trygłow, Trzhiglov, Trylilaw, Trziglov, Trzyglow)

Triglav simply means "three-headed."[200] The statues have been described as having one body with three heads or in one case, depicted with three goats' heads.[201] It's important to remember that Triglav is a composite deity. Triglav is especially revered by the Western Slavs. This deity is supposed to have a throne on the top of the highest mountain in Slovenia, which is called Triglav. The mountain is located in Triglav National Park. The medieval town of Shchechin (Stettin), now known as Szczecin, Poland had a temple dedicated to Triglav.[202] This town is built up between three hills. We also see Triglav in Brandenburg, Germany around 1157 CE. Described as an "idol with three heads… called Triglav in Slavonic…" It was located on a hill with "numerous other idols."[23] Near the town of Daruvar in Croatia is located two villages named Treglava (cf. Trigla) and Trojeglava, likely places where Triglav (or his partner) was revered. In a description by E. Richmond Hodges in 1875 states, "He had three golden heads, each with a hat or mitre, and held the moon in his hand."[18] According to the eleventh century writer, Monachus Prieflingensis, the heads on this xoanon were silver-plated.[203] This has caused confusion over the years because of the association of silver with the moon and gold with the sun. These writers (because of their basis in Greek and Roman mythology) didn't understand that Triglav is connected to the radiance of both celestial bodies.

Monika Kropej explains that one of the variations of this deity's name came from the Roman emperor Trajan who died in 117 CE. Since his name was so similar to that of Triglav, the South Slavs started to use the name Trajan or Traian.[19]

We can judge how old a tradition or the lore is by the symbols they use. The earliest mentions of the God of the Radiant-Life-Giving Sun and his partner are connected with the white chamois goat with golden horns and hooves. (Note, the statue of Triglav depicted with three goats' heads.) Later, the goddess became associated with the cow and in the early development of agriculture a cow or ox was used to plow and to thresh the grain. As the fertility god took on the duties of agriculture, the ox became one of his sacred animals and took on a connection with the sun. The symbol of the radiant white horse comes along later. The earliest mentions of a horse in Slavic agriculture (for threshing) was as early as the "late second or early third century".[204]

Now that you know about Jarilo, Perun/Seibog and Veles you can see him as a triple god under the name of Triglav. Supporting this idea is information recorded by Jožko Šavli. He states the earliest mention of Triglav are "inscriptions found in the place Lagole di Calalzo on the upper Piave in northern Italy [near the border of Slovenia and Triglav National Park]... Discovered inscriptions are in Venetic script, and are dedicated to the holy triad. They portrayed the triad deity as a figure with three heads. They don't name Triglav, but refer to the deity as *"šajnatej"* - the shining one, the holy one."[205] At Lagole, along with the reference to a "shining" deity, there is a sacred site to the "gods of fertility," a hill and pools fed by healing springs used by the Romans for "healing wounds."[206] These three faces of the shining Slavic deity map to the description of the great Nordic Pagan temple at Uppsala which had three images: Thor, Wotan (Odin), and Fricco (Frey). These Nordic deities also map to the seasonal components with Thor and his hammer matching Perun, the god of thunder. There is Wotan, whose name is similar to Weles (Veles) who was revered as the "head god" of the priesthood and is associated with all the dark lore of ravens, wolves and magic. Finally, we have Frey, the shining young lord of spring like Jarilo/Lado.

Followers: *triglavy* (from people in Bulgaria who worshipped Triglav)
Sacred Day, Time or Holiday: Equinoxes and Solstices, December 4th (St. Varvara's Day)

Sacred Space: a hill near a cave (or ravine) and water, watermills

Sacred Animals: goat or mountain ibex *(steinbock)*, ox or bull, black horse, snake

Sacred Plants: shamrock/clover, sassafras, oak

Sacred Objects: tripod, three-legged stool or display, chalice, sword, millstone, scrying bowl, saddle, lighting, a ritual staff with a "T" top, the colors white, red and black as well as blue representing all of them

Offerings: grain, flowers, earth, horns, three candles (or a three-sided candle,) chalice and sword, plant, fruits

Symbol: A triangle pointing up or more recently a triquetra interlaced with a circle

"Flag of Widewuto" from the 6th century CE with Peckols (Veles), Perkūnas (Perun) & Patrimpas (Jarilo)

This rod from the 10th Century was used by the Pagan Clergy of Poland. It has been misidentified as the four faces of Svetovid, when it very clearly shows three faces. The picture comes from the "Illustrated History of Polish Literature" (Lustrowane Dzieje Literature Polskiej) by Henryk Biegeleisen (1855-1935)

Trigla (TRIG-lah) - "The Three-Headed Goddess" - (Treglava)

Around 1700, researcher Benjamin Hederich also suggested that Triglav was a "female deity."[101] This would explain the female version of the name, Trigla or Treglava. In an interesting variation on this tripartite symbolism is preserved in the woman's craft of decorating pysanky eggs. A traditional design of a goddess figure (called a Berehynia) is painted in the center of the egg with a sun above it and a snake symbol called a *zmiya* is below it.[198]

So it may be that there was a female "Triglav" as well which would be composed of Jarila/Vesna/Lada, Perunika/Siva and Mora/Morana/Baba Yaga. Tracing it back we find the Catholic German priest, Hermann Stangefol writing around the year 1600:
"The Paradise Monastery is noteworthy for the fact that it was spared by the enemy in the siege of Soest in 1447... There in an ancient temple, that still exists, there stood there a statue of the Goddess Trigla, which had three heads, to which the pagans in times of greatest need typically ran, pleading for help. It may be thought that it is from this statue [Goddess] that the village derives its name. This statue was destroyed in 1583 during the Cologne War [1583-1588]."[207]

Trigla is not as well remembered as Triglav, since the warrior culture diminished the role of the Goddess and relegated her to the role of daughter, wife and mother. However, Trigla's lore lingered on in other cultures. We see her as the triple goddess, the Morrigan, whose youthful component is Anu, the fertility maiden; Badh, the mother with her cauldron and her dark, crone, death aspect is Macha. The name of Morrigan is used for her three-fold form. Notice that it has the same root as Mora, meaning "dark". This would also explain the origin of the "dark" Greek goddess, Hecate Tricephalos; "the three-headed goddess." Athenaeus states, "At Athens there is also a place called Trigla, and there is a shrine there dedicated to Hecate Triglanthinê."[208] There a fish called *triglas* or *triglê* (which might be red mullet) was offered to her. Hecate Tricephalos is connected to crossroads. She is also associated with Persephone, Demeter and Baubo in the Eleusinian Mysteries.

Followers: *triglavy* (from people in Bulgaria who worshipped Triglav)
Sacred Day, Time or Holiday: Equinoxes and Solstices, December 4th (St. Varvara's Day)
Sacred Space: a hill near a cave (or ravine) and water, watermills
Sacred Animals: goat or mountain ibex *(steinbock)*, ox or bull, black horse, snake, red mullet
Sacred Plants: shamrock/clover, sassafras, oak

Sacred Objects: tripod, three-legged stool or display, chalice, sword, millstone, scrying bowl, saddle, lighting, a ritual staff with a "T" top, the colors white, red and black

Offerings: grain, flowers, earth, horns, three candles (or a three-sided candle,) chalice and sword, plant, fruits

Symbol: A triangle pointing down.

"Hecate" by Talfourd Ely & Hans Dütschke, 1891.

"Radegast & other Gods" from the Chronic der Sachsen circa 1530.

In the center is Radagast, but in the lower, righthand corner is a female figure with three faces, presumably Trigla. It is also possible to distinguish Stribog on the left side with his wings, young Jarilo beside him in armor and in back of Jarilo would be Veles, the Horned God with the Horned Goddess beside him.

Trigla.

"Trigla" by Eduard Sommer, 1835.

Rozhanitsa (Rozh-en-IT-sah) - "The
Birthing Mother", "The Mother Goddess/es and Dispenser of Fate", "The Deer Goddess" (Narecnitsi, Narecznice, Orisnice, Parkas, Rodzanice, Sojenice, Sudice, Sudjenice, Udelnicy, Urisnici, Zaudici)

The name is believed to come from *roditi*, "to give birth."[209] She is ancient, harkening back to the Horned Goddess that was seen over and over on petroglyphs dating back before the last Ice Age, at least 12,000 years ago! It also would explain why her attributes are so muddled. Like the game of telephone, Rozhanitsa's lore has gotten the most confused. She probably started off as just one goddess as we see on the ancient petroglyphs recorded by Professor Jacobson-Tepfer. Eventually she was represented as the three goddesses of fate.

As the Deer Goddess and Mother of the Animals, her embroidered image is often with legs outspread and a child or a little deer between them. She often has the antlers of a deer, or flowers sprouting from her head showing her generative powers. Other depictions show her surrounded by children, sprouting plants, birds and horses.[190] Before she became associated with the deer, she was seen as a female moose (which they call elk in the Slavic lands.) She was seen in her role as the birth giver of the world, bringing life and fertility. Her shamanic followers would carry a long wand (about 44 cm / 17 inches) with a female moose head on the end. It would hang upside down at their waist and then held right-side up in ritual. She is also connected to reindeer.

One of the most magical and miraculous powers of woman is the ability to give birth. This falls in the realm of Rozhanitsa. She is called upon for helping a difficult birth, and taking care of the mother and child afterwards. She would be appealed upon in fertility magic, in potions and spells to ease childbirth and to bless and protect the child and the mother afterwards. What was once a blessing of Rozhanitsa upon a child's cradle, lingered on in a "priestly service book of the seventeenth century, indicating the Christianization of the custom."[210]

Rozhanitsa is paired with Rod, and early Orthodox sermons warned against "offering bread, mead, and cottage cheese to Rozanika and her consort, Rod." Over time Rozhanitsa's power of creation was transferred almost entirely to Rod. By the 12th Century it was recorded in "The Word of Idols" that Rod was the Creator and the Rozhanicy became his wife and daughter.[211] While the birthing goddess goes back to the Paleolithic era, once the Slavic people settled down and had to defend their land from attackers, the god Rod rose to power instead. Christopher Stoop quotes Eve Levin, "[the Virgin] Mary and Rod are similar in that both celebrate miraculous fertility. Thus women celebrated the festivals of the church in honor of Mary, in particular the Nativity of the Virgin on September 8th, by preparing a 'second feast' of bread, honey, cheese, and *kasha* for the Rozhanitsy and Rod. They brought the same foods to a new mother shortly after birth."[210]

The title Sudice means "Givers of Fate." They would seem to be the same as the three Latvian Laimas who spin a person's fate, which connects Rozhanitsa/Sudice to Siva/Laima. In Slovenia we see them recorded as "three fairies": Rojenica, Sojenica, and Babica.[78] The tradition of the Vlach was recorded by Professor Wace in 1914, "Three days after birth they make preparations for the visit of the fates, who come, so they say, at midnight. The child is carefully dressed and one or two gold pieces or some other kind of ornament is hung round its neck. It is believed that if the child is thus decorated the fates will 'write a good fortune for it."[98] They became the Three Fates like the Slovenian Parkas, the Roman Parcae, Greek Moīrai, Hittite Gulšeš, Bulgarian Narucnici, Romanian Moira and Norse Norns.

Some of Rozhanitsa's powers remained in the wild primal woodlands with the goddess Devana, who is also often envisioned with antlers. The fertility aspects of Rozhanitsa as she came down from the north merged with the deep powers embodied the earth goddess, Mat Zemla in the cultures of the South. Somewhere in that mix budded off the motherly Mokosh, as hearth and home became more important. Rozhanitza's daughter aspect merged with the Spring earth goddesses Vesna, Jarila and Lada.

Followers: *moiras or junones*
Sacred Day, Time or Holiday: September 8th (Nativity of the Virgin), The Winter Solstice
Sacred Space: under the stars
Sacred Animals: storks, reindeer, moose, elk, deer
Sacred Plants: evergreens, pine
Sacred Objects: antlers, embroidered cloth, placenta or caul, emeralds, the planet Venus, wand made of antler with female moose head
Offerings: bread, salt, honey, cheese, butter, *kasha*, *kutia*, mead, wine, candles, cookies shaped like reindeer

"Rushnyk" with Mothers, circa 1920.

"The Three Fates" by Hans Baldung - Metropolitan
Museum of Art, 1513.

"The Norns" by Mary H. Foster, 1901.

Rod (rohd) - "The Sky Father", "The Primordial God" (Chrodo, Crodo, Crodone, Hrodo, Krodo, Prabog, Praboh, Rid, Rohd, Sud) -

Rod literally means "kin"[95] and many Rodnovery practitioners have taken this to mean that he is the "Prabog," the "first god." The Proto-Indo-European root of the word *rod*, meaning "kin" or "clan," also generated the titles of king, as well as queen (as in the Sanskrit *rajan* and *rajni*.) This has led people to note a possible connection to the Indian god, Rudra, a primordial god who is worshipped as creating the Universe. However, Rudra goes back only about 4,000 to 5,000 years, while Rod and his partner Rozhanitza go back at least 12,000 years to before the last Ice Age. Some insular Pagan groups interpret Rod to mean only their white Arian kin from the same country as them. This is a sad distortion of the concept that means all humankind. The word *rod* meaning "kin" developed from the older root word of *rozdat*, "to give birth."[188] So it is the primordial goddess who was the creator.

Rod has also been referred to as Div, which goes back to our Proto-Indo-European roots of *dievas*, the "Sky Father." Because these are all titles, we can see the confusion that arises.

In the Sermon of St. Gregory from the 15th century he refers to *both* Div and "the rod." Researcher Alvarez-Pedrosa records the relevant part, "The

Slavic people also offer sacrifices to the same gods, to Vil, to Mokos, to Div, Perun, Khros, the *rod* and the *rozanicy*, to the vampires and to the *Naiads* and the *Pereplut* and they drink to honour him, and they pray to the fire Svarozit and they prepare a bath for the dead and they make bridges and springs, and they make cakes and they practice many other entertainments."[212]

This hints that "the *rod*" may be a triple form of the god, the same as "the *rozanicy*." It also makes more sense to connect the name "Div" to Seibog with his names of "Devac" and the proto-Indo-European origin of "Dievs." Yet, we can see here where it would seem at one point these were all just titles for the same deity, but eventually became worshipped as different deities.

Rybakov, one of the respected names in Slavic Paganism, interpreted Rod as being practically the same as the God of the Bible. Turning Rod into the "supreme creator" despite overwhelming archeological evidence that the birthing goddess was seen as such for many millennia. Rybakov even hung on to this idea to the point of seeing the capped figure of the Zbruch xoanon depicting Vit and Vita, as a huge phallic symbol of Rod! Regrettably, this male-centric view has been repeated over and over. As scholar Leo S. Klejn points out, "not one of the sources directly mentions any such deity..."[213] He proposed that the name of Rod arose from an incorrect reading of some late Greek astrological manuscripts mentioning the Greek word for "genealogy." However, since we know there are the three Rozhanitsy who blend with Siva, it would make sense that there are the three Rod, which would equate to the spring, summer and winter components of Seibog. They would represent a male guardian for the three stages of masculine life: a youth, a father and an elder.

As a more authoritarian figure, his title is Sud, meaning "Judge"[214] which would seem to fit with the idea that the Rozhanitsy are the Goddesses of Fate. Researcher Joannes Richter cites Bothe's Saxon Chronicle of 1492 where he writes about the Romans a millennia and a half ago, who identified Krodo with their god Saturn.[215] Rod and Rozhanitza could connect to Saturn as they share the same holy days around the Winter Solstice. Saturnalia was celebrated from December 17th to December 23rd, and the Rozhanitsy were celebrated on "Mothers' Night" or *Modranicht* at the Winter Solstice. This night is sacred to the *Matres* or *Matronae*. These "Mothers" are found all over Rhineland, Gaul and Britain in the form of three carved women figures. While not depicted as "maiden", "mother" and "crone", but as three women or as two older women and one younger. Yet you must keep in mind that the "maiden" goddess is freely sexual, and the "crone" goddess is still perceived as a birthing mother in her regenerative capacity. In the days when women may not have lived that long, one could be a grandmother and still having children. So it is possible that this is a depiction of the goddess in her triple form.

This brings us to the much less frequent depictions in the same areas of the mysterious "hooded Spirits" also called *Genii Cucullati*. These male "hooded" figures have been compared to phallus shapes with the "hood" of the foreskin. Lest you see this as too much of a theoretical stretch I'll call your attention to the small bronze statue found in Picardy, France where the top face and hood can be removed to reveal a large phallus underneath. While none of these *Genii Cucullati* have been found with inscriptions there is one mention on an imageless border stone "To the Fathers," found in Plumergat, France.[216] Researchers Lambert and Bernier see these "Fathers" as deities guarding the boundaries of the land.[217] This would make them the *Termini* or *Deivoi Termonioi*. Now when we go back to Slavic lands we can find in eleventh and twelfth century texts the word *rod* being used to generally designate "family," "clan," tribe," and "nation."[214] So it can mean those related to each other by common ancestry *or* fealty. As Researcher S. H. Cross wrote, "Throughout the Slavic languages, the primary meaning of *rod* is the yield of fields and crops, then the increase of the family (hence ultimately "birth")... Rod is accordingly the god of fertility and good fortune in the life he creates."[214] Rod is the father of all life.

To add to our understanding, the *Matres* are called the *Matronae Senonae* and also the *Senones*. This means "The Old Ones". This gives us another layer of meaning. The "Mothers" and the "Fathers" are seen as ancestors looking over us. We are their children and they provide for us, help guide us in justice and welcome us back into their arms in death. This is why an extra place for ancestors (the "Mothers" and the "Fathers") is set at the table during the Winter Solstice (Christmas) feast.

Rod is a loving father figure and all the people in the world are his children. The gifts of nourishing grain, fruits, flowers and as well as the animals of the land are his gifts to us. He presents himself in various forms depending on how we need to connect with him at various stages of our life. He is the Radiant Lord and the Giving God. As our ancient ancestors would pray after the Winter Solstice feast, "let all good things be born"![218]

Followers: *genll* or *rod* (spirits that protect the home)
Sacred Day, Time or Holiday: Saturday, Winter Solstice
Sacred Space: tribal lands, village or nation
Sacred Animals: snakes, frogs, fish
Sacred Plants: evergreens, flowers

Sacred Objects: bracelets, hooded cloak, phallus, seeds, legal scales, iron nails
Offerings: grain, meat, bread, eggs, *kutia*, cheese, milk, honey (bloodless sacrifices)

"Priapus" found in Rivery, Picardy, France in 1771. Described as a "deity clothed in a *'cuculus'*, a Gallic coat with hood, and may be an example of the *Genii cucullati*".

"*Genii Cuculatti* & Goddess" Roman relief sculpture in the Corinium Museum, Cirencester; an area of England that is rich in discoveries of carvings of "The Mothers". There they are called *Suleviae*, with a clear connection to the radiant Celtic Goddess, Sulis who is connected to healing hot springs, wells and pools.

the Author:

Patricia Robin Woodruff's maternal heritage is a little known ethnicity called Lemko, one of the highlander groups of the Carpathian mountains. They are also referred to as Carpatho-Rusyns, "White Russians" or Rusyny. She is fondly called "Paraska" by her Lemko relatives.

Woodruff is an artist, an Interfaith minister of Earth Religions, a priestess of Stone Circle Wicca and a spirit-initiated Lemko *bosorka*. She has a Masters of Divinity and a PhD in Metaphysical Theology. She specializes in the ancient religions of the Slavic lands, also referred to as "Old Europe". Her intensive study on this subject has led to some ground-breaking discoveries.

Her upcoming Roots of Slavic Magic Series are serious books for adults, while her youth series is found under "Baba's Secrets of the Old Ways."

https://patriciawoodruff.academia.edu

Author of:
The Prince with the Golden Hand:
Book 1 of Baba's Secrets of the Old Ways

Slavic Magic Moon Meditations

<u>The Call of the Spectacled Owl: An Artist's Journey thru History, the Amazon, and Spirit (with Travel Tips)</u>

<u>Strange Tales of Floyd County, VA</u>

Guided Meditation -
Buyan Island and the Tree of Life: https://youtu.be/Gkg8OGnQ6OA

Bibliography

1.   Applegate, A.U.K., The Date of Mitrovdan (November 8) and Serbian Lore regarding the First Day of Winter and the "Master of Wolves", in Amor Et Mortem. 2014.

2.   Tille, A., *Yule and Christmas: Their Place in the Germanic Year.* Transactions of the Glasgow Archaeological Society, 1899. **3**: p. 426-497.

3.   Znayenko, M.T., On the Concept of Chernebog and Bielbog in Slavic Mythology. Acta Slavica Iaponica, 1993. **11**: p. 177-185.

4.   Gadowskiego, J., *Przeglad Powszechny*. 1891, Krakow: Druk WL. L. Ancyzyca i Spolki.

5.   Horosko, L., *A Guide to Byelorussian Mythology.* The Journal of Byelorussian Studies, 1966: p. 68-79.

6.   Ralston, W.R.S., The Songs of the Russian People. 1872, Ellis & Green: London.

7.   *Henbane*, in *WebMD*. 2020: webmd.com.

8.   Journal of the British Archaeological Association. Vol. VI. 1750, London: Henry G. Bohn.

9.   Leland, C.G., *Gypsy Sorcery and Fortune Telling*. 1889, New York: Charles Scribner's Sons.

10.   Prichard, J.C., Researches Into the Physical History of Mankind. Vol. 3. 1841: Sherwood, Gilbert, and Piper.

11.   *Lion*. Schools Wikipedia Selection - Mammals 2007 [cited 2020 5 June]; Available from: https://www.cs.mcgill.ca/~rwest/wikispeedia/wpcd/wp/l/Lion.htm.

12.   Pavlovic, G., *Cockerel and Lion*, in *Old European Culture*. 2017: OldEuropeanCulture.

13.   Zaroff, R., Measurement of Time by the Ancient Slavs. Studia Mythologica Slavica, 2916. **XIX**: p. 9-39.

14.   Copeland, F.S., *Slovene Folklore.* Folklore, 1931. **42**(4): p. 405-446.

15.   Delights of the Daisy: The tiny flower with huge charm that's entranced artists for centuries, in Country Life. 2018: CountryLife.co.uk.

16.   Chodzko, A., The Prince with the Golden Hand, in Fairy Tales of the Slav Peasants and Herdsmen. 1896, George Allen: London.

17.   Šavli, J. *Kresnik*. 2011 [cited 2019 14 July, 2019]; Available from: https://thezaurus.com/kresnik/.

18.   Hodges, E.R., *The Slavonians, or Slaves.* Anthropologia, 1876: p. xcm - civ.

19.   Kropej, M., *Supernatural Beings from Slovenian Myth and Folktales*. 2012, Ljubljana: Scientific Research Centre of the Slovenian Academy of Sciences and Arts - ZRC Publishing.
20.   Šmitek, Z., Kresnik: An Attempt at a Mythological Reconstruction. Studia Mythologica Slavica, 1998. I: p. 93-118.
21.   Kropej, M., The Horse as a Cosmological Creature in the Slovene Mythopoetic Heritage. Studia Mythologica Slavica, 1998. I: p. 153-167.
22.   Stredowski, M., The Sacred History of Moravia, in Memoirs of Literature. 1722, R. Knaplock: London.
23.   Słupecki, L.P., *Slavonic Pagan Sanctuaries*. 1994, Warsaw: Institute of Archaeology and Ethnology, Polish Academy of Sciences.
24.   Houtzagers, H.P. and et.al., Dutch Constributions to the Fourteenth International Congress of Slavists, in Ohrid. 2008: Radopi.
25.   Trstenjak, D., *Kerons and Ger*. Lives Journal, 2017. **4**.
26.   Brlic-Mazuranic, I., *Croatian Tales of Long Ago*. 1922, New York: Frederick A. Stokes Co.
27.   Hlobil, K., *Before You*. 2009: Insomniac Press.
28.   von Ulrich, A., *The Religion of Our Forefathers II. The Slavonic Races*. Transactions of the Annual Congress of the Federation of European Sections of the Theosophical Society, 1907: p. 155-181.
29.   Bailey, W.F., The Slavs of the War Zone, 1857 - 1917. 1917, London: Chapman & Hall, Ltd.
30.   Kakaševski, V. *Krišnji*. Staris Sloveni 2020 [cited 2020 5 June]; Available from: http://www.starisloveni.com/English/Krisnji.html.
31.   Shaw, P.A., Pagan Goddesses in the Early Germanic World. 2011, London: Bristol Classical Press.
32.   Monaghan, P., Rhode, in Encyclopedia of Goddesses and Heroines: Revised. 2014, New World Library: Novato, California.
33.   *Kouretes & Daktyloi*. Theoi 2020 [cited 2020 10 May, 2020]; Available from: https://www.theoi.com/Georgikos/Kouretes.html.
34.   Dziejan, D., Slavic Deities from Poland (Part 2): Goddess Lela, in Lamus Dworski Blog. 2017: lamusDworski.wordpress.com.
35.   Struk, D.H., in *Encyclopedia of Ukraine*. 2016, University of Toronto Press: Toronto, Canada.
36.   Narbutt, T., Dzieje Starozytne Narodu Litewskiego (The Ancient History of the Lithuanian People). Vol. 1. 1841, Września, Poland: Pisałam w Szawrach.
37.   Yonge, C.M., *History of Christian Names*. Vol. 2. 1863: Parker, Son, and Bourn.

38.   Šeškauskaitė, D., *The Plant in the Mythology.* International Journal of Complementary & Alternative Medicine, 2017. **9**(4).

39.   Goodwin, E., *Translating England into Russian*. 2020, London, England: Bloomsbury Academic.

40.   Kokare, E. *A Survey of the Basic Structures in Latvian Mythology*. Folklore abt. 1991 [cited 2019 10 December, 2019]; Available from: http://www.folklore.ee/rl/pubte/ee/bif/bif1/kokare.html.

41.   Torino, On the Venerable Bede, Jastarnia, Yesterday and Facing the Past or Future, in In Nomine Jassa, Torino, Editor. 2015: jassa.org.

42.   *jutrzenka*, in *Bab.la*. 2020: en.bab.la.

43.   Larson, E., The Best Baby Names Treasury: Your Ultimate Naming Resource. 2008, Naperville, IL: Sourcebooks, Inc.

44.   Stamatovic, A., *Old Slavic Gods*. Scribd.com, 2015: p. 1-84.

45.   Paplauskas-Ramunas, M., *Woman in Lithuanian Folklore*. 1952, University of Ottawa: Ann Arbor, MI. p. 315.

46.   Applegate, A.U.K., Biljini Petak i Djurdjevdan: Vestiges of Serbian Paganism in St. George's Day Celebrations that Welcome the Start of Summer, in AmorEtMortem.Wordpress.com. 2015.

47.   Borissoff, C.L., Non-Iranian origin of the Eastern-Slavonic god Xŭrsŭ/Xors*. Studia Mythologica Slavica, 2014. **XVII**: p. 9-36.

48.   Hoddinott, R.F., Early Byzantine Churches in Macedonia & Southern Serbia: A Study of the Origins and the Initial Development of East Christian Art. 1963, London, England: MacMillan and Co. Ltd.

49.   Bezovska, A. *Brooms: Beliefs and rituals, proverbs and songs.* Radio Bulgaria 2018 17 July, 2018 [cited 24 November, 2018; Available from: http://bnr.bg/en/post/100715090/brooms-beliefs-and-rituals-proverbs-and-songs.

50.   Kossatz, A. *Jańske rejtowanje*. Sorbian traditions and customs abt 2019 [cited 2019 9 July, 2019]; Available from: https://www.cottbus.de/en/guests/sorbian_traditions_and_customs/janske_rejtowanje.html.

51.   Day, E., *Llewellyn's 2014 Sabbats Almanac*. 2013, Woodbury, MN: Llewellyn Worldwide, Ltd.

52.   Andruszewski, G. and J. Godal, Maritime skills and astronomic knowledge in the Viking Age Baltic Sea. Studia Mythologica Slavica, 2006. **IX**: p. 15-39.

53.   Kregzdis, R., East Slavic Gods of Kievan Rus: Stribog (Comparative Analysis of the data of the Slavs Sky and Baltic Mythological systems). 2010. **XIII**: p. 221-232.

54.	*Orans*, in *Symbol Dictionary*. 2018: SymbolDictionary.net.
55.	Saunders, C. and P.J. Allen. *ORANS - the Slavic Mother Goddess (Slavic Mythology)*. Godchecker 2014 5 Dec, 2017]; Available from: http://www.godchecker.com/pantheon/slavic-mythology.php?deity=ORANS.
56.	Ransome, H.M., The Sacred Bee in Ancient Times and Folklore. 1937, London: George Allen & Unwin.
57.	de Gubernatis, A., *Zoological Mythology*. Vol. II. 1872, London: Truebner & Co.
58.	Gimbutas, M., *The Living Goddesses*. 1999, Berkeley, California: University of California Press.
59.	*Gobnait*, in *She Knows*. 2020: SheKnows.com.
60.	O'Riordan, M. *St. Gobnait - the Patron Saint of Bees and Beekeeping*. 2016 13 February, 2016 [cited 2018 31 January]; Available from: https://www.irishexaminer.com/lifestyle/outdoors/gardening/st-gobnait--the-patron-saint-of-bees-andbeekeeping-381607.html.
61.	Blažek, V., Latvian Ūsiņš 'Bee-God and Patron of Horses'. Baltistica, 2012. **XLVII**: p. 359-366.
62.	Bopp, P.F., A Comparative Grammar of the Sanscrit, Zend, Greek, Latin, Lithuanian, Gothic, German, and Sclavonic Languages. Vol. III. 1850, London: James Madden.
63.	Frazer, S.J.G., The Golden Bough - Book II - Killing the God. 1900, London: Macmillan and Co, Ltd.
64.	Parkes, V. *A Cycle of Life and Death: Slavic Goddesses Morana and Vesna*. Ancient Origins 2016 10 November, 2016 [cited 2020 4 June]; Available from: https://www.ancient-origins.net/myths-legends/cycle-life-and-death-slavic-goddesses-morana-and-vesna-006984.
65.	Beresnevičius, G., Chronicles of M. Strijkovsky list of Lithuanian gods. Metai: Lithuanian Writers' Union Monthly, 2006. **No. 8-9 (August September)**.
66.	Vaitkevičius, V., *Studies into the Balts' Sacred Places*. BAR International Series 1228. 2004, Oxford, England: John and Erica Hedges Ltd.
67.	Ginsburg, C., *Ecstasies: Deciphering the Witches' Sabbath*. 2004, Chicago, IL: University of Chicago Press.
68.	Olson, D.P., Artemisia Moontime Elixir: A Recipe for Dream Magic, in Gather Victoria. 2018: GatherVictoria.com.

69.   The American Heritage Dictionary Indo-European Roots Appendix, in The American Heritage Dictionary of the English Language. 2020.

70.   Gwei-djen, L. and J. Needham, Celestial Lancets: A History and Rationale of Acupuncture and Moxa. 1980, London, England: Routledge.

71.   Varahi, D., Feast of Our Lady of the Thunder Candle, in Danavarahi.uk. 2015.

72.   Frank, R.M., Shamanism in Europe? Part 2, An Essay in Collective Memory and Cognition, Bears & Badgers, Basque & Celtic. 2017, The University of Iowa. p. 115.

73.   Kropej, M., Cosmology and Deities in Slovene Folk Narrative and Song Tradition. Studia Mythologica Slavica, 2003. **VI**: p. 121-148.

74.   Griffen, T.D. Deciphering the Vinca Script. 2007.

75.   Escobar, E. *Russian Roots in the Mile High City*. 2015 6 January, 2015 [cited 2018 13 February]; Available from: https://www.wheretraveler.com/colorado/russian-roots-mile-high-city.

76.   Kojic, A. *Dažbog – The Slavic God of Fortune, Wealth and Son of Fire in the Sky*. Slavorum 2017 [cited 2017 6 August]; Available from: https://www.slavorum.org/dazbog-the-slavic-god-of-fortune-wealth-and-son-of-fire-in-the-sky/.

77.   Radosavljevich, P., *Who Are the Slavs? A Contribution to Race Psycology*. Vol. II. 1919, Boston, Massachucetts: R.G.Badger.

78.   Čok, B., V siju mesečine:Ustno izročilo Lokve, Prelož in bližnje okolice. Studia Mythologica Slavica, 2012.

79.   Čausidis, N., Dažbog in Malalas' Chronicle and His Relations with Other Medieval and Folkloristic Sources. Studia Mythologica Slavica, 2000. **III**: p. 23-42.

80.   *Celtic Belenos and Balto-Slavic Veles*. The Atlantic Religion: A 'Prisca Theologia' of European Paganism 2014 11 June, 2014 [cited 2017 20 August]; Available from: https://atlanticreligion.com/2014/06/11/celtic-belenos-and-slavic-veles/.

81.   Tasić, N., Historical Picture of Development of Early Iron Age in the Serbian Danube Basin. Balcanica, abt. 2005. **XXXV**: p. 7-22.

82.   Serith, C. *Proto-Indo-European Goddesses*. Pie Religion 2007 [cited 2018 5 March]; Available from: http://piereligion.org/pantheon.html.

83.   Dziejan, D., Slavic gods described by Stanisław Jakubowski, part 8/20: Zywia, in Lamus Dworski Blog. 2017: lamus-dworski.tumblr.com.

84.   Parihar, P. *Vedic Origin of Slavic Culture*. P Parihar 2016 23 May, 2016 [cited 2018 23 January]; Available from: https://pparihar.com/2016/03/04/vedic-origin-of-slavic-culture/.
85.   Leland, C.G., Etruscan Roman Remains in Popular Tradition. 1892, New York: C. Scribner's Sons.
86.   Tuite, K., *The Meaning of Dael. Symbolic and Spatial Associations of the South Caucasian Goddess of Game Animals*. Linguaculture: Studies in the interpenetration of language and culture. Essays to Honor Paul Friedrich, 2006: p. 164-188.
87.   Šmitek, Z., What do Birds Sing? On Animal Language in South Slavic Folklore. Studia Mythologica Slavica, 2017: p. 111-144.
88.   Dimitz, A., History of Carniola: From Ancient Times to the Year 1813. 2013, Xlibris Corporation: Kindle.
89.   Hathaway, B., The Great Goddess Devi, in Smithsonian Magazine. June 1999.
90.   Shaw, J. *Sulis, Celtic Sun Goddess of Healing and Prophecy by Judith Shaw*. Feminism and Religion 2013 16 June, 2013 [cited 2017 3 October]; Available from: https://feminismandreligion.com/2013/06/16/sulis-celtic-sun-goddess-of-healing-and-prophecy/.
91.   Belenus, in Encyclopaedia Britannica. 2020.
92.   Reshke, M. *Horns*. Spells and Magic 2017 [cited 2017 21 December]; Available from: http://www.spellsandmagic.com/horns.html.
93.   Gimbutas, M., *The Slavs*. 1971: Praeger.
94.   Leeming, D.A., *The Oxford Companion to World Mythology*. 2005, Oxford University Press, Inc.: Oxford.
95.   Rudy, S., Contributions to Comparative Mythology: Studies in Linguistics and Philolopy, 1972-1982. 1985: Walter de Gruyter.
96.   Ilieva, A. and A. Shtarbanova, Zoomorphic Images in Bulgarian Women's Ritual Dances in the Context of Old European Symbolism. The Journal of Archaeomythology, 2005. 1(1): p. 2-12.
97.   Shepping, D.O., *Myths of Slavic Paganism*. 2014: Akademicheskii proekt.
98.   Wace, A.J.B., The Nomads of the Balkans, an account of life and customs among the Vlachs of Northern Pindus. 1914, London: Methuen & Co. Ltd. 410.
99.   Zaroff, R., Organized Pagan Cult in Kievan Rus'. The Invention of Foreign Elite or Evolution of Local Tradition? Studia Mythologica Slavica, 1999. II: p. 47-76.

100.   Chadwick, H.M., *The Oak and the Thunder-God.* Journal of the Royal Anthropological Institute of Great Britain, 1900. **30**: p. 22-44.
101.   Znayenko, M.T., The Gods of the Ancient Slavs: Tatishchev and the Beginnings of Slavic Mythology. 2016, Bloomington, IN: Slavica Publishers.
102.   *Introduction to Lithuanian Paganism.* The Church of the Divine Earth 2018.
103.   Zaroff, R., *The Origins of Sventovit of Rugen.* Studia Mythologica Slavica, 2002. **V**: p. 9-18.
104.   Dragnea, M., The Thraco-Dacian Origin of the Paparuda. Brukenthalia Acta Musei, 2014. **4**.
105.   Handwerk, B. *Worship at Zeus's Birthplace Predates the Greek God.* National Geographic News 2008 25 January, 2008 [cited 2018 24 January]; Available from: https://news.nationalgeographic.com/news/2008/01/080125-zeus-altar.html.
106.   Tooke, W., *History of Russia.* Vol. 1. 1800, London, England: A. Straban.
107.   Yoffe, M. and J. Krafczik, *Perun: The God of Thunder.* Studies in the Humanities: Literature-Politics-Society, ed. G. Mermier. Vol. 43. 2003, New York: Peter Lang.
108.   Beresnevicius, G. *Lithuanian Religion and Mythology.* 2018 [cited 2018 30 January]; Available from: http://viduramziu.istorija.net/socium/pagonybe.htm.
109.   Milošević, N. *Old Slavic Gods.* Enchanted Stream 2017; Available from: http://enchantedstream.webs.com/oldslavicgods.htm.
110.   Zguta, R., Russian Minstrels: A History of the Skomorokhi. 1978: University of Pennsylvania Press.
111.   Dixon-Kennedy, M., Encyclopedia of Russian & Slavic Myth and Legend. 1998, Santa Barbara, California: Abc Clio.
112.   Činga, E. *Midsummer Celebrations in Lithuania: The Magical Night of Joninės.* Like a Local Guide 2015 23 June, 2015 [cited 2017 12 September]; Available from: http://www.likealocalguide.com/blog/midsummer-celebrations-in-lithuania-the-magical-night-of-jonines/.
113.   Lithuania's Happy Paganism, in Survive the Jive. 2015: YouTube.
114.   *Lamia.* Behind The Name 2019 16 November, 2019 [cited 2020 11 June]; Available from: http://www.behindthename.com/name/lamia-1.
115.   Sanidopoulos, J. *Holy Martyr Agrippina of Rome.* Mystagogy Resource Center 2017 23 June, 2017 [cited 2017 5 August]; Available

from: https://www.johnsanidopoulos.com/2017/06/holy-martyr-agrippina-of-rome.html.
116.		Petroff, L., Magical Beliefs and Practices in Old Bulgaria. Midwest Folklore, 1957. **7**(Winter): p. 214-220.
117.		Tuite, K. St. George in the Caucasus: politics, gender, mobility. 2017.
118.		Panayiv, O., Gods of Slavic Mythology, in Ukraine Magazine. 2017: wumag.kiev.ua.
119.		*Slavic Goddesses Vesna and Morana*. Meet the Slavs 2014 13 May, 2017 [cited 2017 7 August]; Available from: http://meettheslavs.com/slavic-goddesses-vesna-morana/.
120.		Torino. *Polish Gods Part III*. In Nomine Jassa 2014 4 October, 2014 [cited 2017 19 August]; Available from: http://www.jassa.org/?p=4598.
121.		Fiske, J., Werewolves and Swan-maidens, in The Atlantic Magazine. 1871: theAtlantic.com.
122.		*Mora*. Succubus 2014 20 October, 2014 [cited 2017 30 November]; Available from: http://www.succubus.net/wiki/Mora_(mythology).
123.		*Clifton Shakespeare Society*. The Academy and Literature, 1895. **48**(26 October, 1895).
124.		Parshall, P.W., et al, Origins of European Printmaking: Fifteenth-century Woodcuts and Their Public. 2005, New Haven, CT: Yale University Press.
125.		*Slavic Peoples Celebrate Korochun (Winter Solstice)*. Russkiy Mir Foundation 2012 21 December, 2012 [cited 2017 24 December]; Available from: https://russkiymir.ru/en/news/130808/.
126.		*Slavic Gods*. Slavia Land 2018 [cited 2018 14 February]; Available from: http://slavialand.org/slavicgods.htm.
127.		Flowers, S.E., *Wendish Mythology*. 2015, Bastrop, Texas: LODESTAR.
128.		Kakaševski, V. *Horz/Khors (Old Slavic Gods)*. Enchanted Streams 2017 20 March, 2017; Available from: http://enchantedstream.webs.com/oldslavicgods.htm.
129.		Karras, A. *Greek Dance: An Ancient Link - A Living Heritage*. 2019 [cited 2019 March 17, 2017]; Available from: http://www.helleniccomserve.com/greek_dance.html.
130.		Korsun, P. *Zaporizhzhya Sights*. Ukraine Kiev Tour 2019 [cited 2019 29 January]; Available from: https://ukraine-kiev-tour.com/ukraine_zaporizhzhya_sights_khortytsia_zaporizhian_sich.html.

131.   Kaldellis, A., Enthnography After Antiquity: Foreign Lands and Peoples in Byzantine Literature. 2013, Philadelphia, Pennsylvania: University of Pennsylvania Press.

132.   Šavli, J. *Korant*. Thezaurus 2012 9 November, 2012 [cited 2018 20 August]; Available from: https://thezaurus.com/korant/.

133.   *Kurentovanje*. Slovene National Benefit Society 2020 [cited 2018; Available from: https://www.snpj.org/slovenian-culture/kurentovanje.

134.   Warwicker, M. *Are we ready to embrace the Michaelmas goose once again?* BBC 2012 29 September, 2012 [cited 2017 4 December]; Available from: http://www.bbc.co.uk/food/0/19731413.

135.   Crump, W.D., The Christmas Encyclopedia. 2013: McFarland.

136.   Ciglenoǒki, S., Late Traces of the Cults of Cybele and Attis. The Origins of the Kurenti and of the Pinewood Marriage ("Borovo Gostüvanje"). Studia Mythologica Slavica, 1999. **II**: p. 21-31.

137.   *Kybele*. 2017 [cited 2018; Available from: https://www.theoi.com/Phrygios/Kybele.html.

138.   *Mat Zemla*, in *World Heritage Encyclopedia*. 2017, World Hertitage Enclopedia.

139.   Lurker, M., A Dictionary of Gods and Goddesses, Devils and Demons. 1987: Routledge.

140.   Haney, J.V., An Introduction to the Russian Folktale. 1999, Armonk, NY: M.E. Sharpe, Inc.

141.   Jones, P. and N. Pennick, *A History of Pagan Europe*. 1995, New York, NY: Routledge.

142.   Welsford, E.E.H., *Serpent-Worship (Teutonic and Balto-Slavic)*, in *Encyclopedia of Religion and Ethics*, J. Hastings, Editor. 1917, Charles Scribner's Sons: New York.

143.   Marjanić, S., The Dyadic Goddess and Duotheism in Nodilo's The Ancient Faith of the Serbs and Croats. Studia Mythologica Slavica, 2003. **VI**: p. 181-204.

144.   Balsys, R., For Baby, Bubble, Origin and Functions. Klaipedos University, 2004: p. 28-45.

145.   Pavček, T., *Čas duše, čas telesa : drugi del*. 1997, Ljubljana, Slovenia: Knjižna zadruga.

146.   Strmiska, M. and V.R. Dundzila, *Romuva: Lithuanian Paganism in Lithuania and America*, in *Modern Paganism in World Cultures: Comparative Perspectives*, M.F. Strmiska, Editor. 2005, ABC CLIO: Santa Barbara, CA. p. 241-298.

147.	Hastings, J., Nature (Lettish, Lithuanian, and Old Prussian), in Encyclopaedia of Religion and Ethics. 1917.
148.	O'Brien, G.K. *Pagan Lithuania*. Draugas 2008 15 May, 2008 [cited 2017 2 October]; Available from: http://www.draugas.org/news/pagan-lithuania/.
149.	Vaitkevičius, V., The Main Features of the State Religion in thirteenth-century Lithuania. 2004. p. 331-356.
150.	Virloget, K.H., Caves and Entrances to the World Beyond, from Where Fertility is Derived. The Case of SW Slovenia. Studia Mythologica Slavica, 2015. **XVIII**: p. 153-163.
151.	*Valaam Island*. Russian Geography 2018 [cited 2018 6 May]; Available from: http://russiangeography.com/Fennoscandia/valaam-island.
152.	Gimbutas, M., *The Lithuanian God Velnias*, in *Myth in Indo-European Antiquity*. 1974, University of California Press.
153.	Anichkov, E., Old Russian Pagan Cults, in Transactions of the Third International Congress for the History of Religions. 1908, Clarendon Press: Oxford, London.
154.	Grivins, V., *Latvian Rock Art*. At The Edge, 1997. **No. 8**(December): p. 22-25.
155.	Grossman, J.D., *Feminine Images in Old Russian Literature and Art*, in *California Slavic Studies*. 1980, University of California Press: Berkeley, California. p. 33-70.
156.	Jakobson, R., *Selected Writings*. Vol. VII. 1985: Walter de Gruyter.
157.	Witczak, K.T., Ze Studiów Nad Religia Prasłowian. Slavia Occidentalis, 1994. **51**: p. 123-132.
158.	Gliwa, B., Witches in Baltic Fairy Tales. Onomasiology Online, 2003. **4**.
159.	Pallua, J.V., What Can the Mythical Frog Tell Us? The Symbolism and Role of the Frog in History and Modernity. Folklore, 2019. **77**: p. 63-90.
160.	Krensky, S., *The Bogeyman*. 2007, LernerClassroom.
161.	Anonymous. *The Myths and Legends of Baba Yaga - The Wise Witch from Slavic Folklore*. Myth*ing Links 2019 [cited 2019 3 June]; Available from: http://www.mythinglinks.org/BabaYaga.html.
162.	Stankiewicz, E., The Slavic Languages: Unity in Diversity. 2015, Walter de Gruyter.
163.	Johns, A., Baba Yaga: The Ambiguous Mother and Witch of the Russian Folktale. 2004, New York: Peter Lang.

164.	Johns, A., The Image of Koshchei Bessmertnyi in East Slavic Folktales. SEEFA Journal, 2000. **V**: p. 7-24.
165.	Wiener, L., Anthology of Russian Literature: From the Tenth Century to the Close of the Eighteenth Century. 1902, New York: The Knickerbocker Press.
166.	Cross, S.H., *The Russian Primary Chronicle; Laurentine Text*. 1377, Cambridge, MA: Crimson Printing Company.
167.	Coulter, C.R. and P. Turner, *Varpulis*, in *Encyclopedia of Ancient Deities*. 2013, Routledge. p. 610.
168.	Hastings, J., *Encyclopaedia of Religion and Ethics*. 1908, New York: Charles Scribner's Sons.
169.	Gaietto, P., An Iconography of Western Religions: From the Paleolithic to Modern Times. 2017: Lulu.com.
170.	Bell, J., Bell's New Pantheon: Or Historical Dictionary of the Gods, Demi-gods, Heroes and Fabulous Personages of Antiquity. Vol. II. 1790, London: British Library.
171.	Curtin, J., Myths and Folk-Tales of the Russians, Western Slavs, and the Magyars. 1903, Boston: Little, Brown, and Company.
172.	Motz, L., The Winter Goddess: Percht, Holda, and Related Figures. Folklore, 1984. **95**: p. 151-166.
173.	Noble, V., *Dakini: The Goddess Who Takes Form as a Woman*, in *Goddesses in World Cultures*, P. Monaghan, Editor. 2011, Praeger: Santa Barbara, California.
174.	Rigoglioso, M. *Stregoneria: The 'Old Religion' in Italy from Historical to Modern Times*. 2000 [cited 2020 13 February 2020]; Available from: http://www.stregheria.com/Marguerite.htm.
175.	Granvil, R., The Esoteric Codex: Demons and Deities of Wind and Sky. 2017: Lulul Press.
176.	Filotas, B., *Pagan Survivals, Superstitions and Popular Cultures*. 2005, Toronto, Canada: Pontifical Institute of Mediaeval Studies.
177.	SiZ. *Dzien Sw. Łucja*. 2016 6 December, 2016 [cited 2019 12 December, 2019]; Available from: http://www.swieta.biz.pl/dzien-sw-lucji/?fbclid=IwAR0mftb1hu5wJnfAntwIHIKTxw_D0Hk34fLtCzsmkzQ5XNCJ11VOx-wjgJl.
178.	Tura. *Beekeeping: Forum New York Beekeeping*. Beetira 2010 15 July, 2010 [cited 2018 5 January]; Available from: beekeeping beetira.

179.   Morrison, W.J., Lithuania's Museum of Ancient Beekeeping. Bee Culture, 1995(August): p. 447.
180.   Munro, H.H., *The Rise of the Russian Empire*. 1900, London, England: Grant Richards.
181.   Rolek, B. *How Eastern Europeans Celebrate New Year's*. The Spruce 2016 30 November, 2016 [cited 2017 8 August]; Available from: https://www.thespruce.com/how-eastern-europeans-celebrate-new-years-1136792.
182.   Merisante, M. *Cloths of Fate: Inter-weavings of Finnic Goddess Embroidery with Ancestry and Mythology*. 2016 20 May, 2016 [cited 2017 28 October]; Available from: https://www.academia.edu/26236183/Cloths_of_Fate_Inter-weavings_of_Finnic_Goddess_Embroidery_with_Ancestry_and_Mythology.
183.   Vasmer, M., Mokosh, in Etymological Dictionary of the Russian Language. 1962, AST.
184.   Lesiv, M., The Return of the Ancestral Gods: Modern Ukrainian Paganism as an Alternative Vision for a Nation. 1978, London, England: Queen's University PRess.
185.   Monaghan, P., Mokosh, in Encyclopedia of Goddesses and Heroines: Revised. 2014, New World Library: Novato, California.
186.   Pallua, J.V. A Newly Discovered Figurative Representation of the Mythical Baba- "Old Baba Vukoša" in St. Mary's Church of Gračišće in Istria. in Sacralization of Landscape and Sacred Places. 2018. Zagreb: Institute of Archaeology.
187.   Mencej, M., Connecting Threads. Folklore, 2011. **48**: p. 55-84.
188.   Gamkrelidze, T.V. and V.V. Ivanov, Indo-European and the Indo-Europeans: A Reconstruction and Historical Analysis of a Proto-Language and Proto-Culture. 2010: Walter de Gruyter.
189.   *Water Wells and Local Customs*. Turisticka Zajednica Opcine Priviaka 2018 [cited 2018 6 December]; Available from: https://www.privlaka-tz.hr/en/privlaka/curiosities-legends#ScrollPage03.
190.   Kelly, M.B., Goddess Embroideries of Eastern Europe. 1989, McLean, NY: Studiobooks.
191.   Kakasevski, V. *Mokoš*. Stari Sloveni 2018 [cited 2018 6 December]; Available from: http://www.starisloveni.com/English/Mokos.html.
192.   Hilton, A., *Russian Folk Art*. 1995, Bloomington, Indiana: Indiana University Press.

193. Markovych, P., Rusyn Easter eggs from Eastern Slovakia. 1987: Braumüller.
194. *Time to Marry: The Pokrov Image*. Russian Icons 2015 18 October, 2015 [cited 2018 12 February]; Available from: https://russianicons.wordpress.com/tag/protection-of-the-mother-of-god/.
195. Maliszewski, R., *Mythology - Perun's Day*, in *Ryszard Maliszewski - Olkusz...*. 2017: zcalegoswia2.blogspot.com.
196. Ilmatar. *Michaelmas - twice*. The One Ring 2015 9 November, 2015 [cited 2017 23 October]; Available from: http://newboards.theonering.net/forum/gforum/perl/gforum.cgi?do=post_editlog;post=883071;guest=188505140.
197. Oulton, R. *Michaelmas Bannock*. Cooks Info 2006 2 December, 2007 [cited 2017 23 October]; Available from: http://www.cooksinfo.com/michaelmas-bannock.
198. Petrusha, L. *Berehynia*. Pysanky 2017 [cited 2017 27 October]; Available from: http://www.pysanky.info/Symbols_NEW/Pagan_Gallery/Pages/Berehynia.html.
199. in Online Etymology Dictionary. 2020: Etymonline.com.
200. Mouravieff, B., *The Beliefs of the Pre-Christian Slavs*. 2003: Praxis Research Institute, Inc.
201. Grimm, J., *Teutonic Mythology*. Vol. II. 1883, London: George Bell & Sons.
202. Alkman, *Slavic Pantheon*, in *The Pagan Files*. 2006: alkman1.blogspot.com.
203. Zochios, S., Slavic deities of death: Looking for a needle in the haystack, in New researches on the religion and mythology of the Pagan Slavs, P. Lajoye, Editor. 2019, Lingva: Lisieux, France. p. 69-98.
204. White, L.T., *Medieval Technology and Social Change*. 1962, London, England: Oxford University Press.
205. Šavli, J. *Triglav*. Thezaurus 2011 30 August, 2011 [cited 2017 26 September]; Available from: http://www.thezaurus.com/webzine/index573c.html?/webzine/triglav/.
206. *Calalzo di Cadore: archaeological spa naturalistic area of Lagole*. Magico Veneto 2017 [cited 2017 29 September]; Available from: https://www.magicoveneto.it/Cadore/Calalzo/Calalzo-Lagole.htm.
207. Torino, Chapels in the West, in In Nomine Jassa. 2017.
208. Athenaeus and C.B. Gulick, *The Deipnosophists*. 1941, London, Engalnd: G.P. Putnam's Sons.
209. Máchal, J., *The Mythology of All Races*. Vol. III. 1918, Boston, Massachucetts: Marshall Jones Company.

210.	Stroop, C.A., *Muscovite Women in Religion*. 2003, Muncie, Indiana: Ball State University.

211.	*Mothers of the World (Ladies of Fertility)*. Traditional Russian Costume 2019 [cited 2019 12 December]; Available from: http:// traditionalrussiancostume.com/embroidinfo/xru_en.php?nametxt=2.

212.	Alvarez-Pedrosa, J.A., The Reconstruction of the Pre-Christian Slavic Religion and Iranian Lexcal Borrowing: A Methodological Review. Ollodagos, 2014. **XXX**: p. 61-80.

213.	Klejn, L.S., *Soviet Archaeology: Trends, Schools, and History*. 2012, Oxford, England: Oxford University Press.

214.	Cross, S.H., Primitive Civilization of the Eastern Slavs, in The American Slavic and East European Review. May, 1946. p. 51-87.

215.	Richter, J., Traces of Vit, Rod and Chrodo. circa 2020.

216.	Davies, W. and et.al., The Inscriptions of Early Medieval Brittany (Les Inscriptions de la Bretagne du Haut Moyen). 2000, Celtic Studies Publications: Andover and Aberystwyth.

217.	Beck, D.N. *Goddesses in Celtic Religion: The Matres and Matronae*. Brewminate 2009 11 February, 2017 [cited 2020 1 June]; Available from: https://brewminate.com/goddesses-in-celtic-religion-the-matres-and-matronae/ (

218.	Łosko, H., Rodzima wiara ukrainska (Native Ukrainian Faith). 1997.

Made in United States
Troutdale, OR
12/27/2023

16484315R00149